HEADSUP4HTS

HEADSUP4HTS

Supporting purposeful school leadership

JAMES POPE & KATE SMITH

1 Oliver's Yard
55 City Road
London EC1Y 1SP

2455 Teller Road
Thousand Oaks
California 91320

Unit No 323-333, Third Floor, F-Block
International Trade Tower
Nehru Place, New Delhi – 110 019

8 Marina View Suite 43-053
Asia Square Tower 1
Singapore 018960

Editor: Amy Thornton
Senior project editor: Chris Marke
Cover design: Wendy Scott
Typeset by: C&M Digitals (P) Ltd, Chennai, India
Printed and bound by CPI Group (UK) Ltd, Croydon, CR0 4YY

Library of Congress Control Number: 2025939803

British Library Cataloguing in Publication data

A catalogue record for this book is available from the British Library

ISBN 978-1-0362-0804-2
ISBN 978-1-0362-0803-5 (pbk)

Contents

About the authors

James Pope has worked in education for 20 plus years. Since resigning from his post as a headteacher in 2018 he created Inspireducate and founded the HeadsUp4HTs community. With a passion for school leadership, education, vision and strategy he works with schools around the world as a coach, mentor and thought leader. Through the founding of the HeadsUp4HTs network he has also become something of an expert in headteacher well-being, working with and influencing organisations and policy-makers.

Kate Smith is a former primary headteacher and ICF accredited coach who has supported thousands of school leaders across the UK and beyond through her values-driven coaching, facilitation and peer support work. A passionate advocate for intentional well-being, sustainable leadership and authentic communication, she specialises in coaching leaders through the rollercoaster ride of headship. Through her work with HeadsUp4HTs, Kate is influencing how the system supports and sustains the people at its heart.

About this book

School leadership has always been a joyful role. To lead a community of young people and adults is a privilege – one which provides leaders with the opportunity to inspire fellow human beings on a daily basis. Those who step into leadership positions do so with a passion and a vision for school and educational leadership. They have a purpose and an intent born of their own experience of education and of teaching and learning; for most that purpose can be distilled down to one simple focus: *to make a difference.*

However, school leadership is also extremely challenging. A world with ever-increasing expectations and reduced resources means that many leaders can be overwhelmed by the operational demands they face every single day. The short-term success of the school has taken priority, driven by the high-stakes accountability culture which pervades the education system in England (and indeed is replicated in other jurisdictions, albeit with different drivers). It can be increasingly challenging for leaders to find the time and the energy for the visionary and strategic – to be proactive. Instead, their days are beset by constant and complex problems that eat up all of their time and prevent them from connecting to their purpose.

It is little wonder then that education is experiencing a recruitment and retention crisis in regard to those prepared and willing to become and stay headteachers.

It is in recognising that the role is both joyful *and* challenging that we can change the culture that surrounds leaders, enabling us to be more intentional about how we support them to *be the leaders they set out to be.*

Based on the experiences of the thousands of leaders within the HeadsUp4HTs community, this book describes the drivers behind the current culture, and the highly impactful actions leaders can take to ensure that they stay connected to their purpose and, as a consequence, feel fulfilled and nourished, with a high sense of well-being.

PART 1

Heads up for headteachers

1

The mission and purpose of the HeadsUp4HTs community

Creation and evolution

The HeadsUp4HTs community has evolved significantly since its creation in January 2019. This was in the time before the pandemic and, while many things have changed since then, in many ways much remains the same, especially in the world of education and especially for headteachers.

In January 2019 a small but determined group of school leaders came together in a school in Liverpool to share their experiences of headship and to reflect on two things:

1. what a privilege and a joy it is to be a headteacher; and
2. how challenging, and in some cases damaging, it can be to be a headteacher.

At that stage there was no plan – and indeed there hasn't been since – but there was a consensus that there was a lack of system-wide support for headteachers beyond the wealth of training available on 'how to be a school leader' *and* that the culture in the system was culpable in making the lives of some headteachers thoroughly miserable.

Initially, we set out to resolve a particular issue. Why is it that the system treats some headteachers with such contempt to the point whereby those headteachers are forced out of their role? Between the four of us in that meeting we had been contacted by numerous headteacher colleagues who had shared with us some fairly toxic stories about how they had lost their job, often as a consequence of the accountability system. These were good people who had bravely stepped into the role of headship and had fallen victim to a system which demands much, often in areas beyond the capability of a school leader to influence, and then throws them on the scrapheap when they fail to solve some of the complex issues that occur as a result. We were angry!

This is an issue that still besets the system today, but it is rarely discussed or addressed. Often it is because the process by which headteachers are forced out neatly sidesteps school policy. It broadly goes like this:

1. a reputationally damaging event occurs, OFSTED, results, *or* a trust takes over a school;
2. a scapegoat is needed;
3. life is made intolerable for the headteacher;
4. the headteacher is called to a meeting by their employer, often accompanied by their union representative;
5. an agreement is reached and the headteacher is quietly 'disappeared'.

It would be nice to think that this slightly immoral behaviour is rare; however, between us we could recount numerous stories from headteachers who had contacted us to share their story. They were often afraid to do so, having signed a non-disclosure agreement which felt threatening and essentially silenced them. In pretty much every case these headteachers had no prior warning, their performance management reviews were positive and they had received no indication that their job was at risk (in one spectacular example a headteacher was asked to pack their bags one week after they had had a very positive performance review with their trust employer).

Many of these headteachers are left psychologically damaged, with huge impacts on their self-esteem and self-belief. They leave the system never to return. These are good people, in whom the system has invested huge amounts of resources in supporting them to take on their role as a headteacher.

As a result of the fact that this all happens behind closed doors, it is not discussed broadly and the system pretends that it doesn't happen very often and is a small and insignificant issue.

Why are we telling you this? Well, it informs everything we do at HeadsUp4HTs – the fact is that this could happen to any of us, at any time. We accept the responsibility of school leadership and the accountability that comes with it, but surely we deserve better than this.

As a result of the meeting we resolved to do two things:

1. to continue to offer support to headteachers who find themselves in this position with the aim of helping them to repair their self-esteem and self-confidence and to support them in getting 'back on the horse', either through finding another headship, by getting back into education in a different role or by supporting them to do something entirely different. We call this our *crisis coaching*. Sadly, we still get a slow but constant stream of these calls every week, and we are not the only ones supporting headteachers in this space (Headrest is another example);
2. to shine a spotlight on this issue to the Department for Education (DfE) with the support of the school leaders' associations.

Regarding point 2, fast forward eight months and we are back in Liverpool holding our first event with around 30 school leaders; all had been through a version of the above, all were prepared to some extent to share their story. Our aim, to hold a series of events in a Jarrow March-esque attempt to build some momentum, with events to follow in Birmingham and, finally, London. We wanted to shame the system into addressing this issue.

In March 2020 we had set up our second event in Birmingham with approximately 200 people signed up … and then the country went into lockdown. Rather than abandon the event altogether we switched to an online space. On a sunny Saturday morning people joined this event to share their story and to support and lift each other up. It was so successful that we ran another event the following week, and the next, and the next – and we continue to hold this space for school leaders on Saturday mornings and Wednesday evenings to this day.

Beyond headteachers

It has evolved into a space not just for those of us that have suffered the loss of our jobs, but for anyone who seeks support, connection and the need to be 'lifted'. Importantly, they are spaces that are psychologically safe, confidential, free from judgement and, despite the sharing of challenges and difficulties, nearly always joyous.

From this was born a key aim for us as a community … can we make one headteacher feel better about themselves on any one day? If we can, we have fulfilled our mission.

It was during this phase of our evolution that we started to coin the phrase 'for headteachers, past, present and future'. We are called HeadsUp4HTs, but we wanted to be clear that we are here to support the well-being of those that have been headteachers, those that are headteachers and those that will be. When we use the word headteachers in this book it means all of these things!!

In a reflection of this important principle, this book is intended in the same way. You may be a headteacher of significant experience, you may have just started, you may not be a headteacher any more but have been one in the past or you may be at any point on a journey towards headship.

In fact, the ideas, strategies and actions outlined in this book are actually nothing to do with headship per se ... they are about how we can look after ourselves and each other better as human beings devoted to the world of education.

After the pandemic our community continued to grow, slowly at first, reaching 500 at some point in 2020, but then more rapidly with some 10,000 plus members in summer 2024.

Local networks and emerging principles

James was increasingly being asked by local authorities, headteacher associations and trusts to deliver keynotes on leader well-being to headteachers. It was through this work that the HeadsUp4HTs network evolved further – alongside our national network, could we create small local networks using the peer support methodology? We will be forever grateful to Jane Ratcliffe (formerly of Oxfordshire and now in Redcar and Cleveland) for persuading us (against our own beliefs) to give it a go in Oxfordshire. Since then we have created peer support networks in some 35 local authority regions across the country, all of them underpinned by some emerging principles:

1. we take off our 'cloak of invincibility' (more on this later) and leave our egos at the door;
2. we listen;
3. we celebrate each other;
4. we support each other;
5. we respect the experiences of everyone in the room;
6. we think about ourselves as human beings first and headteachers second; as a consequence, we discuss the impact on *us* rather than the technical/operational aspects of leading a school community.

We also found ourselves developing some core principles around how we can better support headteachers in their role.

1. Intentionality

Our starting point had been the crisis coaching; however, this work was at best reactive and at worse definitely fell into the 'shutting the stable door after the horse had bolted' arena.

Could we become more front-footed in the way we support headteachers with their emotional well-being and could we therefore help them to lower stress, lower anxiety and to find more joy in their role ... so when the difficult moment arrives they are better prepared to thrive afterwards?

Could we (and the system) be more *intentional* in our approach to supporting headteachers?

2. Sustainability

Coaching is brilliant, both in the personal and professional space. We are big fans! However, there are some significant issues in providing coaching for all 24,000 plus headteachers, trust leaders and other assorted leaders in the system.

a. The money doesn't exist and it is wholly unlikely that the DfE is going to fund system-wide coaching support for school leaders – partly because there is no additional funding and partly because once you start to fund it you can't stop. Coaching is not a one-off hit; it is an ongoing commitment to self-reflection and improvement ... It is a career-long endeavour.
b. Headteachers are highly unlikely to spend money on coaching for themselves in a world where they are constantly fighting to balance the books. That's not to say that coaching is not available in some schools, local authorities and trusts, which creates a further issue ...
c. Inequity. In a world where some are receiving coaching and others aren't, it is inevitable that some school leaders will be better placed to face and overcome the challenges of the role than others. This is highly likely to be impacted by size of school and budget and local funding formulas – that is, headteachers of small primary schools are less likely to have the funds available to justify an annual spend on coaching for themselves or their team. That's not to say they shouldn't

(we strongly believe they should), but we accept that it is not a personal decision and that permission needs to be given by someone else.

d. Availability of coaches. The reality is that there are not enough coaches to go round and we have discovered through our support of some 4,500 school leaders that headteachers, especially, appreciate being coached by someone who has been or is a headteacher ... someone who 'gets it'.

To address these issues we decided that *sustainability* is key – that is, can we ensure that our peer support and coaching methodologies create the conditions whereby school leaders can self-sustain the support long after they have worked with us?

The community

Finally, a word about the community. We are a network organisation first and foremost. We don't pretend that we have all of the answers to leader well-being. However, what we do have is a huge insight into the issues that our very human school leaders are facing in their roles and it is these insights that inform what we believe the solutions to be. The strategies and actions that we outline in this book stem from those issues and are tried, tested and adapted by each individual member of our community.

What we hope is clear from the above is that our work with headteachers is based on principles that have evolved over time to enable us to provide effective and impactful support for school leaders at scale. However, when we reflect on our work, daily, weekly, termly, annually, our key question remains the same: 'Have we helped one school leader feel better about themselves and the impact they have?' If we have, then our mission is fulfilled.

We celebrate and support headteachers while campaigning to change the culture in the system to one of intentional, sustainable support, thus enabling all headteachers to flourish and thrive in their role and for them to have lengthy and fulfilling careers.

A bit about context

Each of us go about our daily business, being the best that we can be. The role of school leadership is demanding enough to keep us focused inwards and it is rare that we have time to look up with the capacity to see what is happening to those headteachers around us, never mind what is happening at a national level.

A question we ask ourselves all of the time is 'Why are we needed?' Another way to think about this is 'What issue are we trying to resolve?'... this helps us to avoid falling into the trap of existing because we think we are needed.

While the numbers in our network who are seeking and benefiting from our support would indicate a need, it helps to have a bigger aim.

In the early days this was solely about stopping the toxic behaviour whereby good headteachers were being removed from their post for nefarious reasons. The main aim is to support those individuals rather than a grand notion to change the world in which this behaviour occurs. However, it helps to have a bigger objective – in this case to get upstream of the issue and stop it from happening in the first place. We believe that we (alongside others) have made some progress on this, partly through calling it out when we see it happening. We know it still happens – we still have to provide crisis coaching – but we can hope that our collective voice calls those employers who behave like this into question.

Similarly, now, alongside the above, our aim is to provide headteachers with effective support and strategies that help them to thrive in their job. This is enough in itself; however, we are also doing our bit to address a system-wide problem. The retention figures for headteachers in their first five years of headship are appalling. The fact of that matter is that too many skilled and experienced school leaders are stepping into headship and then making a conscious decision to step back out again.

In November 2022 the NAHT published 'Gone for good' (NAHT, 2022). Their analysis of school leader retention shows:

- 25 per cent of primary school headteachers leave their position in the first five years of headship – 64 per cent of these leave state education altogether;
- 37 per cent of secondary school headteachers leave their position in the first five years of headship – 67 per cent of these leave state education altogether.

These figures are outside those who leave due to retirement. The report also includes worrying data around the desire of senior leaders in schools to step into headship (and equally worrying retention rates for senior and middle leaders).

Clearly, this is deeply concerning for a number of reasons:

1. these are devoted, determined human beings who have honed their leadership skills over a long period of time and care deeply about education;
2. the system has invested heavily in these leaders over the course of their careers;
3. as well as the obvious loss of skill and knowledge we also lose significant experience and wisdom. The research is clear that headteachers get better at being headteachers the longer they do the job, perhaps an obvious point but one worth making.

The reasons stated are varied and not surprising (long hours, high-stakes inspections, inadequate school funding, lack of autonomy and difficulties in recruiting staff). What is worthy of curiosity is a deeper reflection on the *why*.

School leadership training is arguably the best it has ever been (formally through qualifications or informally through experiential development) so this is not an issue related to a leader's *technical* ability to lead. Therefore, we have to look elsewhere, to be curious enough about the reasons to make sure that we are addressing the right issue and therefore seeking the right solutions. The insights we gain from our network would indicate that it is not the ability to do the job that is the issue; it is the emotional capacity to do the job over an extended period of time. So, our 'higher' purpose beyond supporting individual leaders is to address the issue of leader retention, to make it a job that people believe they can do for a long period of time despite the issues that they might face that are beyond their ability to influence.

Reference

NAHT (2022) *Gone for good: leaders who are lost to the teaching profession.* Available here: www.naht.org.uk/Portals/0/PDF's/Campaigns/NAHT-Retention-rate-report-FINAL.pdf Accessed April 2025.

2

A very personal experience – experienced by many

The culture surrounding school leaders isn't unique; however, there are some unique aspects to it.

Engineering an impression that all is well

One aspect that we explore in detail through our HeadsUp4HTs support methodology is the uneasy tension between the requirement for a headteacher to be a compelling leader – that is, confident, dynamic and capable – and the inner self-reflection and doubt that are entirely human characteristics (they are normal – we are not superheroes!).

This tension exists for all of us; however, for school leaders it is couched within a culture and context whereby schools and the performance of schools is constantly questioned. There is an overarching negative narrative that indicates that we are never quite good enough (more on that later).

It is therefore not that surprising that headteachers have to work hard to engineer a perception that the school is doing well, that education and learning are going well, that they know what needs to be addressed and they know what they are going to do about it. There is a constant fear of failure that drives us to create a world in which we are doing OK.

It is within this context that a serious issue for well-being arises. In order to acknowledge that we need support, we have to acknowledge that we are human and vulnerable. However, all of the people that we are encouraged to turn to for support (governors, senior leadership team (SLT) colleagues, trust leaders) are simultaneously the same people that hold us to account for the work that we do. As a consequence, we don't admit or share our worries, concerns or vulnerabilities as that might somehow lead to the notion that we are 'not coping' or indeed failing as a leader. This is, of course, nonsense, yet it is a very real consequence of the culture that exists in our system.

It should be OK to say that we are not OK

Nevertheless, it is not and therefore we don't. We bravely carry on even when we are aware that the role is having a significantly negative impact on our mental or physical health.

It is for this reason that James shares his own story openly when he is presenting on well-being to school leader groups. It is an important part of the presentation to create the notion to the leaders in the audience that:

1. they might be in a really good place at the moment and that is to be celebrated;
2. they might not be in a really good place at the moment and that is entirely normal.

It is also the case that James' story acts as a warning sign for what might happen to a confident and capable leader if the appropriate support is not provided. Most of us have an inner belief that we are indestructible, until we find that we are not.

In line with the HeadsUp4HTs key principle of intentionality, it's crucial to acknowledge that we can't predict what lies ahead and, while we are pretty good at navigating uncertainty, intentionally developing a set of well-being strategies and tools ready for when challenges arise is just as important as using them when a crisis occurs.

It is for that same reason that we include James' story here in this book. Some of you may know aspects of it already. Part of his story is that he was involved in the BBC 2 series *School* which aired in November 2018. The programme aimed to demonstrate the almost impossible conundrum that headteachers are presented with, to highlight the external issues that headteachers are expected to deal with, without question and often without resources, while they improve the quality of education for young people in their community.

The point here is that James' story is not unique. Hundreds of headteachers have experienced similar challenges and they leave the system as a consequence, burnt out, exhausted or just plain demoralised. Or, as discussed in Chapter 1, forced out of the system.

James' story is a lightning rod for many others and he tells it because many others are not able to. As a system, we know this is happening, we know it could potentially happen and yet we allow it to happen anyway. It is not good enough. By telling it he hopes that it will offer comfort to those that listen that they are not alone in feeling the way that they do, and that if enough people listen, that it will lead to change.

A secondary reason for including it here is that it is as a direct result of his experience that James created/founded the HeadsUp4HTs network. No caring, determined and passionate educationist should have to go through anything similar, but if they do then there should be somewhere or something available to those headteachers so they do not feel alone.

Case study – James' story

In 1997 I trained to be a teacher. I didn't have any particular desire to work in education, it had not been a long-held career aim. In reality, I stumbled into it. At best I endured the college sessions. However, from the moment I stepped into the classroom with my first attempt to deliver a lesson and light the fire of science learning in students, I loved it. For the first time in my own education and working life I had found something that I really enjoyed doing and, to my own surprise, appeared to have some aptitude for it! At the end of my training year I secured a teaching position with my main placement school.

Over the next few years I grew in confidence, buoyed by the impact my lessons were having on students. I guess I was fortunate to be working in a confident organisation surrounded by brilliant colleagues who guided and helped me. I was also fortunate to work for a very inspiring headteacher. Leadership opportunities came my way and I took them. I loved teaching and the craft of teaching, but I also loved pastoral work – I really enjoyed working with kids. I became a head of year, then a head of science and, finally, an assistant headteacher. From those early leadership opportunities grew a desire to be a headteacher – I believed (and still do) that if I could impact on students as a teacher then I could broaden that impact by leading and working alongside my colleagues. If I was to secure a headship I felt I needed more than one school experience; I secured a deputy headship at another school. I continued to learn and develop but my core belief did not change.

(Continued)

I wholeheartedly believe in the power of distributive leadership. For me it is not about how good I am at something; rather that as a leader I can help others to become better at what they do.

Headship, here I come!

After a few failed applications I was successful at Marlwood School. Some context: student numbers had been falling for several years – simplistically this had been attributed to the school not providing a good enough education, resulting in parents sending their children to other schools. While there was an element of truth in this, what had not been looked at in any depth was the local demographic; in short there were not enough students in the area for the school to ever return to the size that it had been in the past. This point is very important for the context of my leadership at the school. The lack of any action or forward planning to address a problem which had been known about since 2008 created a key issue that needed to be urgently addressed and would impact on everything we did, educationally and financially. In December 2013 the school was inspected. The headteacher at the time was absent and the staff did their best in very challenging circumstances with no leadership. The local authority was heavily involved, as was the CEO of an emerging trust. The school secured a 'requiring improvement' (RI) judgement on the understanding that it would join the trust and rapid action would be taken to resolve the issues. The remainder of that academic year would be spent trying to secure the best results possible for Year 11, recruiting a new headteacher, restructuring and working to restore some sense of order prior to the school joining the trust formally in December 2014.

Marlwood felt like a school where I could achieve something; it was clear that the school had endured a difficult few years. At the time of my interview it did not feel as if these would be insurmountable. I was struck by the openness of the staff and the acceptance that something was not right and it had to change – the 'burning platform' was obvious to all and there would not be a need to overcome resistance from the staff body. Completing due diligence while being interviewed over a 48-hour period is nigh on impossible in my experience. The budget, as presented, looked good and there was even some carry forward to help soften the increasingly tight finances. More than that, it felt like a good fit for me, I liked the school, the staff and the students. The fact that it was joining a trust also gave me confidence.

Once I had been offered the job I spent the remainder of that academic year finishing off my work as a deputy and working to get up to speed on my new school. This is a strange period of time in the education world; you feel like you are holding down two jobs, excited about the one ahead and sad to be leaving the one you had.

The start of a new year, I am a 'headteacher'. I have a lot to learn but I have confidence, principles, a vision and a plan:

- *be visible;*
- *build confidence among the staff body;*
- *get the culture right among the student body;*
- *create a culture of development, open doors, sharing good practice, celebrating the positive;*
- *give clarity to leaders and a clear strategic plan.*

There are some key moments when the reality of what you have taken on hits hard, and they come thick and fast – the first INSET day and open evening are two that spring to mind. You are a public figure – get the messages right because everyone is looking to you!

The first year was an absolute whirlwind and I loved it. I got to know the school well; there were lots of positives, as there are any in any school, but there was a hell of a lot to do.

- Teaching and learning. *A decade of education development seemed to have passed the school by, in regard to the curriculum (lacking any plan or cohesiveness), schemes of learning (in places excellent, but in others non-existent – resulting in teachers having to invent the wheel for every lesson), pedagogy (some superb practitioners, but others who had not been invested in and this was reflected in their lessons).*
- Student culture. *Amazing students (aren't they all?), but too many with low aspirations, negative about their school and lacking responsibility for their own learning.*
- Finance. *The budget that had been set in April (as a local authority school) had to be remodelled for the transition to an academy. What became clear, very quickly, was that the budget for the year did not balance. The carry forward had been used to balance the books which created a double whammy. The carry forward was not as much as had been thought (ouch 1) and there was an in-year deficit of £250,000 (ouch 2). Planning forward to the following year also revealed that the fall in student numbers was going to cost us dearly. A point here for clarity, as it was often mis-represented in the press: students were not leaving, they were just not joining. A year group of 200 students leaves Year 11*

(Continued)

to be replaced by a year group of 100 in Year 7. In total – save £1 million by the following September and save a quarter of that in-year.

- Post-16. *Unsustainable: amazingly confident young adults, but too few of them.*

In essence, the school was a mess. We didn't talk about OFSTED, but we agreed as a school that we were RI and that as long as we were improving that would be enough. However, despite the dedication and hard work of many of the staff it was clear that the RI judgement nine months earlier was generous. I wasn't fazed. What it meant was we would need to be creative and radical in our thinking and brutally honest about where we were. We became an academy, governors left, staff left, we relentlessly targeted Year 11 (short term – play the game!), we restructured everything we could and became an outward-facing school learning from our primary partners, secondary partners, locally through the trust and the local authority and further afield through Achievement for All (AFA), London Challenge schools and a teaching alliance.

Writing this down, it's easy, looking back, to stack everything up negatively. However, this was school leadership, the energy was amazing, the challenges were clear; it was an incredibly exciting time. The staff accepted the various challenges and their solutions. We developed a three-year plan, our journey to excellence. Subject areas across the school developed teaching and learning excellence maps that they would hold themselves to account for. Maths and English worked hard with primary partners (who were amazingly generous with their time). They ripped up KS3 schemes of learning and developed new ones with more stretch and challenge based in the reality of what they had seen that the pupils were capable of at KS2. The culture started to shift: a house system, new uniform and clarity around behaviour expectations was having an impact – more so in the younger years, but still an impact to be celebrated. We balanced the books both for the year and for the following year's budget. We ended the year on a high, everything was starting to change.

You don't get a lot of feedback as a headteacher. But at the end of the year the feedback I did get from the community, parents, students, staff, my CEO, partner headteachers and governors gave me the confidence that we were making progress. The strategies were the right ones and were having an impact.

Another headteacher moment – results days, the anxiety, a very public 'proof in the pudding' moment. Post-16 results were OK – not brilliant, but not a disaster. At GCSE a couple of subjects that had previously delivered solid results, bombed. Despite all the intervention for Year 11 the picture was a long way from good. Damn. OK, dust yourself off and go again, Rome was not built in a day. You start to feel the rhythm of your organisation and the school year. New year, new leaf. Students in new uniform. Looking smart, feeling proud. Culturally, it all felt different; the results may not have been there, but this was moving, we were improving, people were smiling!

You welcome the new year, but it is a fleeting moment, before you know it you are planning for the one afterwards. The strategic 'quick wins' are in place and up and running.

Now to nail the big stuff – the curriculum; if we get that right and launch it for the following year we will have done the single most important thing. Attainment at the school had always been OK and sometimes was good, a reflection of our above-average intake. The progress wasn't OK and our curriculum needed to address this if we were ever going to get away from the hamster wheel of Year 11 patch, repair and panic intervention. Our curriculum would be planned to build on the pupils' prior success at KS2, to reflect the above-average nature of our intake, to excite the students and to stretch and challenge them ALL. This is the key stuff for me, it's long term and it is the backbone of your tenure as a headteacher. The curriculum, in its broadest sense – to include the principles, the structure, high-quality schemes of learning, the pedagogical development to deliver it and the extra-curricular. The financial pressure meant we had to be creative, but the educational benefit was more important. Our students deserved the best; they were bright, but they were 'coasting' and our curriculum was going to push them. New GCSEs on the horizon. All of this went into the pot. We looked at what was out there, we researched. We developed something collectively as a school, there were high levels of buy in – we were going to launch the following September, and we needed to be ready. Oh, and the small matter of the finances, those student numbers haven't stopped falling so we need to save, approximately, another £800,000 for next September.

Again, we ended the year on a high. It had been challenging, but the curriculum we had developed had given the whole staff something to get behind. Confidence was up; I had created additional leadership capacity which meant I could contribute to 'the system'. I was chair of the secondary headteachers and became executive headteacher of a trust primary school. The results were up, but progress was still a problem. The books didn't quite balance at the end of the year, so we had a deficit and there had been no way for us to set a balanced budget for the following year, so we were also looking at a future deficit.

The rhythm of the year, Year 3 for me. The added ingredient? We were definitely getting an OFSTED visit this year. We continue to do all things we had in our plan;

(Continued)

we face the day-to-day challenges and celebrate the day-to-day joy. Every Monday to Wednesday we wait for the phone call – 12 noon, breathe, get on with it. It's almost comical, but it's too important to laugh at it.

It comes towards the end of the year. A year in which it felt our momentum was building. Like buses, for me, as executive headteacher of a primary, it came twice. Primary first. Hard; we toughed it out. A primary school that had been struggling for years. Last inspection, special measures. This one we were self-evaluating at RI, but in truth we had changed a lot in 14 months and we had a secret hope of pushing to a good. In the end we got the RI with lots of positives to take forward that the school would be good very soon. A smile, a job well done, a celebration and then back to the planning board. Tick.

Ten days later OFSTED visit two and it was brutal. Day 1 you fight for all you are worth. This is my school this is me. Let me show you what we are. We know ourselves; we are not good; we are RI – progress is our key issue, but we are not below the floor ... we have identified the problem and we are acting. The kids were amazing, the inspection team did not see one single piece of disruption, low level or otherwise, over the two days and they referenced it. By breaktime on day 1, two hours into the inspection, I know we are in trouble as the word 'inadequate' is launched for the first time by the lead inspector. If you have experienced it, you will know the sinking feeling in your gut. They listened to the context, save £2 million in two and a half years and improve the school – interesting, not relevant not in the framework. As I write I this I am looking at my notes from the day 1 'feedback' session and the anger rises in me. It is so surreal; it is so contradictory it isn't what the OFSTED leaders have been saying for the past ten months across the media and Twitter (now X) – the historical data seems to be all that matters in this inspection. When talking about teaching and learning the maths inspector reports that he hasn't seen anything less than good and some excellent practice. The English inspector agrees. Teaching and learning – inadequate. Don't get me wrong – there were things that were not good and we didn't disagree with them, but they were also not surprises to us. This is what our self-evaluation had said. In the end, despite the positive, despite the obvious positive culture displayed uniformly by our students, the die was cast. We were 'inadequate' and it changes everything.

It all came down to the following, perverse and circular argument. In the last inspection the school was RI (as described above, this is highly questionable). The school self-evaluation says RI – therefore you have not improved quickly enough, therefore, you are inadequate.

Inadequate colours everything and you have to rip everything up and start again. As a headteacher it is personal; your school reflects who you are and the report is a reflection on everything you have given in your time at the school. For the remainder of the year you dig deep into your emotional intelligence reserves. Face your public with a mixture of anger and pain, but remain the composed leader at all times. What was a fragile but tangible recovery has been blown out of the water. I think about resigning (self-doubt reinforced by external feedback), but, actually, I believe in what we have done (self-confidence despite the feedback). I talk to staff one to one; I describe the difficult year ahead; I see the fear and the emotion in their eyes and in their body language – it reflects my own ... suck it up, buttercup.

At the same point we, the secondary schools within the trust, have agreed to make a TV programme. So, the 'what happens next' will be visible in a strangely compelling two hours of television to be broadcast on BBC2. In summary, what you will see is the unravelling of everything we had achieved in regard to the culture of the school. The worst moment of the outcome? Having to stand in front of the staff and the students and tell them we are in special measures. When I call the assembly the sense of anticipation is palpable. I know what they are thinking as they sit there in front of me in their perfect uniform: 'Did we get a good*?' For them, the majority of the students, the school has changed beyond recognition; they are happier, their learning is better. When I say it there is an audible gasp in the sports hall – the emotion is real from these kids. I swallow hard to stop my own emotions overtaking me. The parent reaction is similar – anger and upset from those who have not bought into what we have done, but from the quiet majority a series of very supportive emails expressing disbelieve – for many their journey has been the same as their children.*

I resolve to fight and fight hard on behalf of my beloved school. A lot of challenging, difficult and emotionally draining work is done before and during the start of the next academic year.

The year starts, perversely, with the celebration of our best ever attainment results and the welcoming of the first significantly increased number of Year 7 students in six years. We worked hard to manage the messages to those parents who had bought into our philosophy and they stuck with us. Despite what has been reported by local press I can count on the fingers of one hand the number of parents who took students out of the school and stated categorically that it was because of the OFSTED judgement. The rest stuck with us and I am eternally grateful

(Continued)

to them for doing so. The reason they did? What they said was: it doesn't feel *like an inadequate school. My child is happy and safe and they are enjoying their learning. Go figure!*

The year also starts with the same financial pressure, savings required for the next budget equal £970,000. By the end of the academic year 2017–18 the income for the school had reduced from £5.4 million when I was recruited to £2.6 million for the start of the academic year 2018–19. Each and every school has its own challenges, but I would maintain that ours were pretty unique – take a rural, leafy comprehensive that has been neglected for a while and improve the quality of the education while saving £2.8 million in four years. I don't think this is spelt out clearly enough in the TV programmes so I am doing it here.

*In me, though, something has shifted. I am by nature a glass half full person and I have carried that glass right through the last three years. But now the anger and the sense of injustice are taking over. This is compounded as I watch things around me start to disintegrate as a consequence of the outcome. Sadly some of the students will wear the cloak of inadequate very quickly – 'This school's sh*t' – and ongoing pressures are created by staff reductions. We all fight on, but it feels very different. For me there is a rising sense of doom on most days; I can hear in my own head the rising note used in movies to provoke a feeling of impending disaster. I smile, I joke, I try to keep everyone positive, but there is just not enough capacity to deal with everything we need to do. My days get longer, my sleep gets shorter and I watch it all happen on television as I look ill and tired. Monitoring visits? Turned out to be one step forward and two steps back. Apparently, things are improving, but not quickly enough. We were fortunate to be allocated a HMI who was astute and sensitive to our context. Ultimately, though, there is a framework and Marlwood does not fit the framework.*

Despite all of this we ended the year with the books balanced, another OK set of results and a systematic restructure (how many restructures in four years?). The school is set up very well for the future if someone can find a solution to the financial difficulty. The foundations are strong and the succession plan to replace me has left the right leader in place to see it through – I think he will be brilliant. I thank my lucky stars I was in a trust surrounded by brilliant and supportive colleagues, I'm not sure how I would have coped as the head on my own.

This was my reality of being a headteacher in a challenging school. We work in a system where the margins between an inadequate and an outstanding school are quite small. We all know that in our inadequate schools there will be an awful lot of good stuff and some brilliance going on every day, but the term 'inadequate' permeates everything and becomes all-consuming. I know that there will be teachers, support staff and leaders who will have got up this morning and have had to take a big deep breath to face the reality of what is in front of them. As a headteacher? Well, the reality is that when we are asked if we are OK – we all say yes, don't we?

I think the time has come to say 'no'. It's not OK.

People ask me – why did you leave? Well, actually not for the reasons people may assume. I genuinely think we achieved something at Marlwood, but I am self-aware enough to recognise it needed a new energy to see it through. I don't think any big decision we make in our lives is ever for one reason. For me there were a lot of reasons to think that I had done my bit professionally and I needed to invest a little bit in my personal and family life. I loved my job. Without a leadership post I still think of myself as a school leader because that is who I am, riddled with self-doubt and self-confidence. If anyone will have me, I hope to step back into the ring soon.

In the current climate, I am often asked 'Would more money have helped?' Well, yes, of course. I think it is dismissive and ridiculous to be told it is not about the money – this was stated several times to south Gloucestershire headteachers. However, I agree that it is not all *about the money. In fact, what I needed more of was time. I was dismayed by our finances, but I get more dismayed by the short-termism that currently exists in our system.*

There are some key points to highlight. We do so here as an opportunity for individual headteachers to reflect on, but also because it is imperative that we act upon them as a system.

- To what extent does your experience of headship echo or reflect that outlined here? The detail of the challenges may be different, but the impact of the challenges might be the same.
- To what extent are the issues highlighted above beyond reasonable expectation for a headteacher to resolve?
- As James highlights, he was surrounded by supportive people both within the school and across the trust. To what extent might some external coaching support have helped James to remain in headship to avoid the inevitable burn-out that occurred in his last year?

- To what extent might we expect to be able to foresee the emotional consequences and inevitable impact on James' well-being of the challenges he faced at the school?
- If you were advising James at any point in the narrative above, what would you say to him?

Reference

BBC2 (2018) *School.* Available here: www.bbc.co.uk/programmes/b0bs43b7 Accessed April 2025.

3

The joy of school leadership

There are a number of reasons why it is important to start a book about leader well-being with a reflection on what a joyful job/career/vocation it is. We will explore some of those reasons later in this chapter, but for now the most important one is related to a keyword in our mission statement 'celebrate'.

In a world of overt and constant negativity about the work of schools it is easy to fall into the trap of becoming negative about the work that schools undertake every day (more on this in Chapter 4).

The reality is that there is much more to celebrate than there is to be negative about. Schools are far more successful places than anyone casually reading about them would be able to ascertain. So, we should be celebrating more than we do, and it is in this celebration that we can reconnect with the joy of the job. This is a fundamental tenet of our support processes which are explored in detail in Part 2.

Let's start with a statement.

Headship – the best job in the world

We often attribute this statement to Vic Goddard and then get told off by Rae Snape who claims she said it first ... In reality it has probably been coined by many!

> What is your gut response to that statement? Agree? Disagree?
>
> What are your reasons?

This is a good starting point for exploring the joy of school leadership. But it does create a binary response and the reality is it is much more nuanced than that. So ...

Chances are that if you are reading this book you are: a) a school leader (HT, DHT, AHT) or a trust leader (CEO, executive HT, etc.) and b) and that you are somewhere on the spectrum shown in Figure 3.1.

Figure 3.1 Do you like your job?

(If the right-hand box seems overly negative we accept that it is exaggerated to make the point, but it is also important to recognise that for some leaders there may have been times when they did feel like this ... if you have spent any time coaching a HT in crisis you will know that it is not that far-fetched.)

Where you place yourself on this spectrum is a highly personal reflection, the chances are that it can change on an hourly, daily, weekly or termly basis! Let's broadly suggest that you might fall into one of the following three categories:

1. for some it is absolutely a joy to be a headteacher;
2. for many it can be a joy, but it doesn't always feel like it;
3. for some it used to be a joy, but it isn't any more.

In reality for the purposes of this chapter it doesn't really matter whether you agree or disagree with the statement, where you place yourself on the spectrum or which category you fall into (it does become important later on in the book).

The key point is that the exercises above create a situation where you have to think about it and that inevitably leads us to ask some questions. Many of these questions are in the 'why' space:

Why is it the best job in the world?

Why is it joyful to be a school leader?

Wherever you currently are in your relationship with your school leadership position let's explore the why.

To be inspired is great, to inspire is incredible.

Attributed to Napoleon Hill

A small statement that packs a punch and is perhaps a perfect summation of the role of education in everyone's lives.

As young children and then adults in a school environment it is highly likely that at some stage in our education we have experienced the sentiment of the first half of this statement. Most people can recall at least one teacher who was that inspiration. The fact is that pretty much everyone on the planet will have been inspired by someone at some stage in their childhood. It is a great feeling; as school leaders we can probably all recall a specific moment or person who inspired us to step into education, become a teacher and then move on into leadership. It is a part of everyone's narrative, but it is easily forgotten or lost in the mists of time.

For our purposes the important part of the statement is the second half.

To inspire is incredible

In contrast to the first part of the statement, it is not guaranteed that everyone in the world has the chance to inspire others. We *might* get the chance to do so in our friendship groups, if we are fortunate enough to have children, and possibly in our career.

As educators it is pretty much *guaranteed* that we will have inspired people. As teachers, it might be young people in our classrooms, and then, as leaders, young people and staff in our schools and parents in our community. It is a rare job indeed that provides the opportunity on a daily basis for us to inspire someone.

Inspiration is a difficult thing to measure and track; it is rare for someone to tell you that they have been inspired by you. This is often because it is subtle and nuanced; we may not realise that we have been inspired until years later and even then it is unlikely that we will go back and tell that person. It is entirely likely that we don't feel particularly inspirational and we certainly wouldn't describe ourselves as inspirational; that would feel entirely too boastful for people who are by nature self-effacing. It is not our personalities that make us inspirational, it is the cultures that we create in our schools that provide the opportunity for inspiration to happen. There are thousands, if not hundreds of thousands of people who will be affected by this across the country on a daily basis.

We don't *have* to be inspirational; it happens as a consequence of the job and it is a real privilege to be in this position. And, specifically, because we are in this position every single day we can forget or lose sight of the fact that this is what we are doing. Therefore, it is important to remind ourselves.

It is in recognising that this is a privilege that we can find the joy of school leadership. But we have to look for it. Where do we find it?

Well, this is where we start to get into some of the detail of our support processes. Broadly, where you find joy will be directly linked to your purpose, why you do the job. These joyful moments are often small and can seem insignificant to other people (they certainly are to those who judge our schools and the work we do in them). It might be as inconsequential as seeing a child open a door for another child or member of staff; it might be an assembly; it might be watching children in lessons; or in the myriad extra-curricular opportunities that we provide. It can be in watching the hard work and dedication to resolve an issue for a particular young person come to fruition and for that young person to start to shine in your community. The joyful moments are small, seemingly inconsequential, but in complex interconnected human-based organisations the chances are that a large number will be happening all of the time.

When we ask the question 'Where do you find the joy in your job?' of leaders and other staff in schools (and we have done this thousands of times) it is *always* the case that the examples provided will be directly related to an impact on another human being in their community. It is rarely the *big* stuff, no one has yet to provide an answer related to an OFSTED outcome, results or data analysis. That's not to say that those big moments are not joyful, it's just not the reason why we do the job. They are outcomes, not the purpose.

Our purpose is to make a difference for other people; it is a privilege to be able to do this every day of our lives. In the small insignificant moments that is exactly what we are doing.

That's why being a school leader *is* the best job in the world.

4

The challenge of school leadership

So, if we can agree that headship is the best job in the world, why is it that it doesn't always feel like that? Why does it feel so challenging?

As a leader it is entirely possible that when you read the word 'challenging' you have already started to think about how your job is challenging. When we present to groups of headteachers we rarely have to unpick why the job is challenging; there is a general understanding that it just *is*. It is at this point that we show a graph from Scott Belsky on the depiction of the 'real journey' of building a company (image search 'Scott Belsky real journey' online to see the graph).

It is a useful visual representation of what it can be like to be a school leader. When we first become a headteacher it is inevitable that we are at our most joyful 'awesome, let's do this'. Our joy at this point far exceeds the level of challenge that we might be experiencing; this is partly due to naivety (a headteacher in the network three months into their headship lamented 'Why didn't anyone tell me what it would be like?') and partly due to a lack of knowledge or awareness of the breadth or depth of the challenges we might be facing in this new role and (probably) new school; in this regard ignorance is truly bliss!

Fuelled by this joyful energy we begin the process of getting to know the school and the challenges start to become clearer.

Working on the basis that definitions are important let's explore the definition of the word itself:

challenging

adjective

1. *A challenging task or job requires great effort and determination.*
2. *If you do something in a* **challenging** *way, you seem to be inviting people to argue with you or compete against you in some way.*

(Collins, 2023)

The two different definitions give us a useful starting point for exploring the challenge of school leadership.

In the first definition we have a strong sense of being tested. The test will have two dimensions, personal/internal and external. The internal test is especially relevant when we first become a headteacher, but also applies to experienced headteachers stepping up into a new school. The external challenge is likely to be related to the particular circumstances and context of the school that you are leading in.

In the second definition we get a sense of the external world looking in on us, and the weight of expectation that can come with this. In this sense we are experiencing a provocation: 'Can you do this job, can you improve this school?' but there is also a strong underlying sense of judgement.

So, we have three frames through which to explore the challenges of being a school leader:

1. the external 'public' world and the way that it views education in the broader context and our school community more specifically;
2. the specific context and challenges of leading our community;
3. the personal challenge of being a school leader, the test of our own skill set, characteristics and leadership capabilities.

The external challenge

I don't think that anyone reading this or anyone working in our schools is going to deny that education is hugely important, and perhaps the most important thing that a society can do on behalf of its citizens. The effect of excellent education impacts on the individual and on the society in which that individual exists. The power of education at its best is that it has the ability to improve the life of anyone, and also to make all of our lives better by impacting directly and indirectly on the challenges that a society might face. It has the potential to resolve the problems in a society through prevention, therefore reducing the need for cure (an obvious example of this would be public health).

As a consequence of this, any effective government is going to make education a priority (we accept the point that it depends on the particular government as to the extent to which it is prepared to prioritise education; often the impact of effective education can take years to pay dividends and the shorter term the government ideology, the more likely it is to say it values education without actually investing in it).

For headteachers in England this is where the challenge begins. Education is important and it costs a lot of money, therefore we had better make sure that we are getting value for money and that our education system is the best that it can be. A direct result of this is the creation of a regulator to hold the system to account (in England this would be OFSTED). So, we have a government that wants the best education system and a regulator that is created to find out where this is and isn't the case. Throw in a national media that has its own culture of sensationalism and negativity (who wants to read about good news stories!) and the result for the general public is a steady stream of negative and often sensationalised stories about education and schools. The more specific and local consequence of this is often a parent community that is predisposed to think negatively about their local schools (often in spite of the very positive experience their children might be having at the school).

The irony of all of this for those of us that work in education, and especially those that lead our schools, is, of course, that we want a brilliant education system and we want the experience of young people in our schools to be amazing ... the further irony is that the very government that is demanding this from us and then bashing us over the head when we don't deliver it is the same government that is responsible for resolving most of the specific societal and educational challenges that make our job so difficult. One of the most toxic approaches taken by OFTSED in the past two decades was to start using the phrase 'moral imperative' to beat schools over the head with, as if we didn't care! Whether they mean it or not, the implication of the moral imperative narrative is: 'If we, OFTSED, tell them, schools, how important education is, maybe they will stop being lazy and work a little harder' – which in itself is just a more direct version of the culture and approach OFTSED has taken since its inception in its current form.

Give it long enough and this culture will establish in the psyche of society and this creates a more specific external challenge for school leaders related to the way the culture implicitly or explicitly informs the thinking of our parent community. This has been amplified by the rise of social media. Whereas in the past a parent might be unhappy about something that has happened in their child's school, and they may have used this incident as validatory evidence of the culture they have been reading about it in the media, the likelihood is that they would discuss this with close friends at the school gate, in the pub/café or around the dinner table. Now it is likely to be thrown into a social media group where the negativity goes unchecked and is amplified by others.

This has resulted in a very particular cultural environment surrounding our schools and, sadly, it is very much a deficit view. Rather than celebrating all of the great work that our schools do, we exist in a world that is constantly judging and questioning the quality of education and the work of schools.

This agenda and narrative have become gospel, best demonstrated by the term 'improvement'. The word itself is not in itself negative; it literally means to make something better – that thing could already be pretty good! However, in education it has become hijacked by the accountability agenda, where we are told (often in no uncertain terms) that something is not good enough and we had better do something about it and fast) ... from this we form our school improvement plans. Indeed, because we understand the moral imperative so well, we spend a huge amount of time, energy and resources identifying those things that are not good enough and doing all we can to improve them. We therefore spend a significant amount of our time focused on those things that are not working as well as we would like in our schools. It is more often than not the case that these are wicked problems – that is, they are complex, difficult and can often be a result of things beyond our control (e.g. if you have ever tried to 'improve' the quality of maths teaching in a school where you struggle to recruit maths teachers, you will know what we mean!).

The specific context and challenges of leading our community

Compared to the above, the challenges here are easier to manage. At least we have some measure of control over them and some agency in resolving them.

It is useful here to make a blindingly obvious point, but one that is often missed because of the 'snapshot' judgements made by OFSTED. *All* schools are developing all of the time and therefore all schools will have a list of focused priorities that they are working on. Therefore, regardless of the school we become a headteacher in, it is likely that there will be a set of challenges that we want to address. At its most base, they will fall into two categories:

1. challenges related to the culture, behaviour and aspiration of young people;
2. challenges related to the quality of education, the curriculum and its delivery.

In this regard school development is simple! However, the challenges and the approaches that we might take to address them will almost certainly be complex. And the level of challenge we face will be directly linked to the context of the school; a significant part of this context will be the last OFSTED judgement.

Which is where things get interesting (and is the reason why we think there needs to be a significant shift in the narrative that surrounds education, away from an overtly negative one towards one which is more celebratory and positive) ... at no point in the last two decades has OFSTED 'judged' less than 80 per cent of our schools as good/outstanding. The next 10 per cent of schools used to be judged 'satisfactory', but we now labour under the term 'requires improvement' (ridiculous term, show me a school that doesn't think it requires improvement in some areas and, if you can find one, I will show you a school that is probably going backwards!). So, 90–95 per cent of our schools are doing a pretty good job, day in and day out, on behalf of the young people in their community. When you consider that we would universally agree that OFSTED is our harshest critic, you can see why we firmly believe that we need to reframe the narrative into something more positive. The point here is that it is highly likely that you are going to become a leader in a school that is already doing a pretty good job! *But* that doesn't change the fact that you will face challenges in the two areas described above.

It is likely that the challenges that you are facing at this point are not unique to you, but challenges that are being faced across the sector to a greater or lesser extent by everyone. Again, this is where it gets interesting because those challenges will have solutions and those solutions will have been tried, tested and proven. Some of them will come from your own experience, others will come from other leaders and schools in your network. So why can it be so difficult? Again, this is where we have to look externally. Many of the wicked problems we face are not created internally, but by the factors and parameters set outside our schools. That's not to say that there might not be an awful lot of work to do to get the culture and quality of education right, but it is nearly always the case that the resolutions are hamstrung by factors external to your organisation – funding, resource availability, societal issues would be just three.

A further dimension to these challenges is that we implicitly know that the solutions, applied and implemented correctly, may take years to fully deliver and yet we exist in a world where external pressure demands we resolve them quickly (the moral imperative again) which drives us towards a space of short-term 'fix' solutions. The workload, energy demand and capacity required to operate eternally in this short-term space leaves us with little to no capacity to implement the longer-term solutions that will ultimately be better for the organisation and the cultural shift we are trying to deliver. So, we are held constantly in a *reformation* space with little to no capacity to lead to the *transformation* that we know will be more fulfilling. Some of our heads describe this as the hamster wheel.

The personal challenge

'Nothing prepares you for headship' is a statement we hear a lot!

When we start to apply for headships we are almost certainly at a point in our career where we believe we are ready to meet the challenge. It is likely that we have already held significant leadership positions where we have been exposed to a significant amount of experiential learning. We will have completed leadership development programmes and we will have (probably) achieved the NPQH. We will have had a role model headteacher ourselves (for good or for ill) who we will have observed and learnt from. We can therefore be reasonably assured that we are as ready as we will ever be … and yet, we don't know what we don't know. We experience this in two different ways: first of all, we almost certainly don't know the school we are leading in (except in the case of an internal promotion) and, second, we will have not experienced the full breadth and depth of the role. We certainly won't have experienced the unique isolation that is created by the responsibility and accountability of being the ultimate leader of the organisation.

While we believe that we are ready it is also true that there will be doubt. To work in education is to spend an awful lot of time in a reflective space. It starts as soon as we train to teach, where we are encouraged to reflect, evaluate and develop our practice … did that work? What could be developed? What might we do differently? So there is a baked-in tendency to question and reflect (which is a strength). It is also true that people who work in education have a tendency towards self-reflection and self-doubt. While we all have an ego, we know from the extensive work we have done with headteachers that there is a character type, a tendency to be humble.

So, we tend to find there are a number of internalised dialogues that are taking place:

- I'm ready … I'm not ready;
- I'm a compelling leader … I'm a vulnerable leader.

A great way to exemplify the duality of this inner dialogue is to remember back to the point when you were told that you had been successful in your headship application. The first emotion you experienced was probably joyful, you were probably ecstatic that someone else had validated that they thought you were ready too. Then, a short time later, a different set of emotions as the reality sets in: 'Can I do this?' or even 'What have I done?' Let us normalise this ... the greater majority of the headteachers in our network went through the same thought process. It is an entirely human response!

So those are the challenges we might face in our own self-belief at the start of the journey. Then we embark on the job of *being* a headteacher and as described in the 'real journey' along the way there will be 'successes' and 'failures', things we get 'right' and things we get 'wrong'. We have placed these terms in quotation marks because, of course, they are mostly based in self-perception (we'll talk more about success/failure and right/wrong later). These challenges will be specific and unique to us and the context of our school. They will probably be very much born from the operational load of leading a school. It is highly likely that our more challenging moments will come from those areas we are less confident or have less experience in. As we grow as leaders and our experience and wisdom increases, then these operational challenges diminish. It is for this reason that an experienced leader mentor is nearly always a good idea in the first months/year of headship. However, no matter how experienced or wise we are, the breadth and depth of the role means that even when we think we have 'seen' everything the job has a habit of throwing up new and different challenges that we haven't faced before. This can be problematic because, even if we have years of headship experience, it throws us back into the space of self-doubt.

The third area of personal challenge that can develop over time is linked to our sense of purpose and is a crucial element of how we can effectively support headteachers with their well-being. When we made the decision to become a headteacher, we probably had a strong sense of purpose, of what we wanted to do and how we were going to do it. It was probably very much focused on the internal requirements of the school, developing the culture and quality of education. As we experience the job, we start to realise that we spend significant time and energy grappling with the external factors described in the two points above. Then, over time, we might start to think that the time and energy we are devoting in this space feels purposeless. This means we have less time and energy for the purposeful stuff and we may start to doubt not just our ability to do the role, but also the nature of the role in the first place.

Reflection: internal challenges

Issues like competition, the constant pressure from stakeholders and the high-stakes accountability system are significant challenges. Some of these feel imposed by the system and the role itself.

As we've discovered through our work with headteachers, there's another, often hidden, layer to this struggle. It's the internal challenges – the self-limiting beliefs that we carry about what leadership should look and feel like, and our ability to capture and compel a multitude of stakeholders.

As you can imagine, over time, these perceptions of ourselves shape how we feel and how we lead, and can create a gap between who we are and who we think we need to be.

But we don't have to let these beliefs drive us or hold us back. The key lies in reconnecting with what truly drives us, a strategy HeadsUp4HTs is well versed in.

Reference

'Challenging' (2023) *Collins English Dictionary*. Available here: www.collinsdictionary.com/dictionary/english/challenging Accessed March 2025.

5

The issues as described by school leaders – and the drivers for those issues

Much of the emphasis in leadership development in our education system focuses on professional behaviours – that is, our technical ability to lead and manage a school. We hope that you will already have a sense from earlier chapters that our support work focuses very much on the human being who is a headteacher rather than the headteacher who happens to be a human being. When supporting leaders with their well-being, or lack of it, you focus on the human being *first,* as it is here that our sense of well-being is impacted.

In the same way, it would be easy for us to describe the issues that leaders face on a daily basis through the lens of the strategic and operational workload. The problems, sometimes wicked, that we have to resolve on a daily basis, are, in no particular order:

- finance
- behaviour
- SEND
- pupil premium outcomes
- subject performance
- quality of teaching and learning
- curriculum
- technology

- safeguarding
- recruitment and HR
- staffing.

This non-exhaustive list represents some of the biggest strategic issues of our times. Underpinning these challenges are the myriad of avenues through which these issues express themselves in our own school communities. We might call this the *operational load.*

We are obviously as interested in trying to solve these issues as much as anyone else who cares about education. However, there are plenty of spaces where these get considered, discussed and actioned – from our own school staff meetings, to our governors, our trusts, our local authority headteacher groups, training and CPD forums and conferences. We spend most of our professional life grappling with these strategic and operational leadership issues and trying to solve them. The issues are likely to change over time, depending upon the strategic direction and policy implementation of the government of the time.

Where we, as a system, devote less time is to supporting the human beings who are the professionals. At HeadsUp4HTs we are interested in the issues that arise for those humans who are valiantly trying to be the headteacher who solves the endless list of strategic and operational issues in their community – in other words, the human impact.

As a network of several thousand leaders and organisations, we are privileged to get an insight into these human issues – either through individual headteachers who open up and share them with us, through our multiple peer support groups across the country or through our surveys.

Over the past five years, the challenges that are consistently identified as having a negative impact on the well-being of schools leaders are:

1. isolation;
2. impostor syndrome;
3. competition;
4. high-stakes accountability;
5. impact on personal and professional relationships.

These challenges and their impact on individuals are not unique to leaders in the English education system; they also resonate with other educational jurisdictions (e.g. India, Australia, international school settings). Indeed, they are not unique to school leaders; leaders in other sectors have described similar challenges to us.

It is important to us to have a good understanding of these issues as we structure our support for headteachers in response. While there is a generality to the list, it is important to note that each individual leader's experience and context is their own; we might provide each with a scaled score through a well-being survey that helps us to understand how to best tailor our support to suit a particular individual. If we are feeling particularly 'joyful' about our role (see Chapter 3) we might give ourselves a low score – that is, we are aware of the issues, but they are not having a significantly negative impact on our well-being. If we are feeling particularly challenged by our role (see Chapter 4) we might score ourselves quite highly in some or all of the areas because they are having a significant impact on our well-being.

The reason why we make the points above is that we can be assured that, regardless of the particular culture or context that we are leading in either nationally or locally, these are prevailing core issues for leaders. They are *climate* issues rather than *weather* issues.

It is almost certainly the case that, as you read the list, you considered what each term meant for you in your own context, and that is important. It is equally important for us, in working with large numbers of leaders, to be clear about what we mean.

Isolation

Leadership is a fine thing, but it has its penalties. And the greatest penalty is loneliness.

(Ernest Shackleton, cited in McKee, 2020)

This quote is not related to school leadership per se; however, it resonates with school leaders. It's a strange truth for headteachers because in reality, as leaders of very human organisations, we are surrounded by people every single day of our professional lives. Yet, we will all have experienced loneliness, sat in our office, at home or indeed while sat in a meeting at school surrounded by colleagues. We know that there might be lonely times as a leader when we accept the position and the responsibility, but it doesn't make the impact of that loneliness any less challenging when we do experience it.

Leadership can be lonely because leaders are responsible for the successes and failures of a team, project, or organisation.

(Clarke, 2025)

Through thousands of conversations with headteachers, we recognise that isolation does not necessarily stem from being alone or feeling lonely, but rather from the realisation that there are very few people who truly understand your role, the weight of responsibility and accountability (both emotionally and energetically) that comes with the title of headteacher. And, with that, it feels that there are very few people that you can turn to to authentically share the challenges, the highs and the lows without fear of judgement. It is likely that we have a good understanding of what to do to combat this loneliness, but it can be hard to shake the sense that we alone are responsible, we alone are 'carrying the can' – it comes with the decision-making authority that is inherent in leadership positions.

If we are feeling particularly joyful in our role that feeling may be fleeting and not impact us that much. If we are in a particularly challenging moment, then it may be with us all of the time and indeed it might keep us awake at night.

Impostor syndrome

Impostor syndrome, also known as impostor phenomenon or impostorism, is *the persistent inability to believe that one's success is deserved or has been legitimately achieved as a result of one's own efforts or skill* (*OED*, 2023).

This sense or feeling sits with us all. It is interesting that with school leaders it actually comes from a character strength that is common to many headteachers – self-reflection. Not only is it an inherent characteristic in many of us but it is actively encouraged from the very early stages of our career; as teachers, we are constantly reflecting on our lessons, dissecting them and reflecting as to whether we achieved what we wanted to achieve and what we can do to make the lesson better. In Chapter 2 we touched upon the uneasy balance between being compelling – how we present externally to others as leaders – and vulnerable – how we feel internally, the inner dialogues that we all have with ourselves. If we summarise this there are two factors therefore that can contribute to a sense of impostor syndrome:

1. *our internal sense of self-belief*: the extent to which we believe we have the capacity and capabilities to be competent in our job. When we apply for a headship it is probably the case that we feel that we are ready to take the job on, that our prior leadership experiences have prepared us; however, it is equally likely that we have some doubt – after all we haven't done the job yet. What many of us discover pretty quickly is that: a) nothing truly prepares you

for headship and b) it is a hugely diverse job that requires a certain skill level in a wide range of areas, a significant proportion of which could be argued to be outside of our area of expertise – education;

2. *our external feedback loops*: the extent to which we receive positive or negative feedback on the progress we are making in our personal development and the development of our school communities. In Chapter 1 we explored the context of the education system in which we lead and manage our schools. The overtly negative culture that exists around schools does not help us here when we are looking at impostor syndrome. It is not surprising – in a world where we are consistently being told that we are not doing a good enough job on behalf of our young people that then forces us into a space of improvement and what to fix next – that we can often feel that we are not doing a good enough job. It would take an incredible amount of hubris and ego for us to be able to filter this external noise out.

The HeadsUp4HTs view on this is that if we can keep our ability to be compelling broadly in balance with our inner vulnerabilities (amplified by the negative culture) then that probably makes us great leaders – that is, thoughtful, reflective and prepared to admit our mistakes, but also decisive, with a vision for education in our community.

Impostor syndrome becomes an issue because of an imbalance in these two things – when we become so vulnerable that we are unable to lead for fear of getting it wrong (interestingly, the reverse is also problematic – when we become so convinced of our own brilliance and our ability to be compelling that we stop being reflective ... This can lead to 'hero' leadership and is often perceived as being toxic by those we are leading).

Reassuringly, the vast majority of headteachers that we work with will speak of their experience of navigating impostor syndrome. Whether they have been a headteacher for 20 years, or are new to the role, impostor syndrome is a common pattern of thoughts that infiltrates almost every school leader. Understanding the source of your sense of impostor syndrome, then identifying when and why you feel like an impostor and focusing on combating the unhelpful thought patterns, is a way to keep the impostor at bay.

Competition

It is arguable that we have the most collaborative education system in our history. There are networks aplenty in which school leaders can come together to share practice and to work together on development strategies. Alongside this, the multi-academy trust (MAT) agenda has created small, medium and large organisations where collaboration can take place in a more formal setting. And yet our headteachers talk about this uneasy sense of competition that sits just below the surface. If we look at the factors that drive this there are probably three key ones:

1. *OFSTED*: it is obvious that the organisation designed to inform parents and the community about the quality of education that a school is providing also creates a sense of competition between schools in local geographical areas. On one level we might be able to put this to one side; however, in a very real sense a single-word judgement (or indeed a report card) has the consequence of pitting one school against another in regard to some key operational areas (see 3. below);
2. *performance tables*: while the link between school performance and OFSTED outcome has been somewhat severed in the past few years, school performance, which in itself is highly complex and therefore contentious, creates competition in the same way that OFSTED outcomes do;
3. *resources*: in a world in which resources (finance and staff in particular) have become increasingly limited it is no wonder that we can end up in a highly competitive space. We always use the example of schools in a similar area trying to recruit maths teachers!

It is a sad reality that the headteacher down the road from you is facing the same challenges, yet we rarely have the time to reach out to them for support through fear of judgement, ego and a loss of bums on seats for funding reasons.

High-stakes accountability

Much has been written about the culture surrounding accountability in our education system, and every one of us will have fairly strong opinions about OFSTED. It is important to note that, of the thousands of leaders in the HeadsUp4HTs network, none of them shirk their responsibility and all of them accept accountability. In fact, headteachers have become increasingly adept at holding themselves to account with their governors and trust colleagues (see impostor syndrome). Headteachers do not have a problem with accountability; it is the high-stakes nature of our accountability system that is the problem. Also, the high-stakes nature of the system is interesting from a well-being perspective because the impact on leader well-being is two-fold:

1. the accountability system (OFSTED) and the fear that your job might be on the line if your school does not 'perform' well in an inspection creates a highly pressured environment for leaders, not just during the inspection, but in the run-up to inspection and in the aftermath;
2. it has an amplifying effect on the other four factors – that is, it can increase our sense of isolation, it can amplify our sense of impostor syndrome, it is a key factor in competition between schools and it can have a negative effect on our professional and personal relationships.

Impact on personal and professional relationships

It is perhaps not surprising that our headteachers discuss how their own well-being (or lack of it) can impact on their professional and personal relationships. Education is a vocation and, therefore, it is implicit that we are personally invested as well as professionally invested. In most roles that we might have in our schools we are able to keep some separation between these two things. But being a headteacher is a deeply personal endeavour. The schools we lead become a reflection of our values, our personalities and the very essence of who we are as human beings, and we invest everything we have in them. A consequence of this is that it can be very hard to put the job down, even when we recognise that there is a detrimental impact on our own well-being and our relationship with those we care about in and outside the school community.

It makes sense then that if we are feeling particularly challenged in our role and our well-being suffers as a result, this will have an impact on our professional relationships within our school community. It equally makes sense that the pressure we might be feeling is taken home and this might impact on our relationships with family members.

The way we are at home impacts on the way we show up at school, and the way we show up at school, impacts on the way we show up at home …

Reflection: others feel the same way too

The HeadsUp4HTs sessions made me feel normal about how difficult some of the situations I was addressing were. This helped to address the impostor syndrome I was feeling. Despite being a headteacher for some time, I had no idea others were affected in just the same way that I was.

References

Clarke, G. (2025) *Leadership can be a lonely place.* Available here: www.reached.co.nz/leadership-a-lonely-place/#:~:text=A%20leader%20is%20required%20to,a%20team%20or%20an%20organization Accessed April 2025.

McKee, J. (2020) *Loneliness and leadership ... a post from the past.* Available here: www.linkedin.com/pulse/loneliness-leadership-post-from-past-john-mckee/ Accessed April 2025.

Oxford English Dictionary (OED), s.v. impostor syndrome (n.), September 2023. https://doi.org/10.1093/OED/3742536120

6

What is well-being?

We have no doubt that you will have a broad understanding of this term; at the very least you will be very aware of the concept of well-being and of the increased focus on this term in our society over the past few years – especially in the post-pandemic era.

As a leader it is highly likely that you will be conscious of it on behalf of the young people and staff in your school. You will have almost certainly undertaken a well-being survey with your staff, which may have had the ironic effect of negatively affecting your own well-being!

We take a real interest in the term; if we are going to address well-being in an intentional way it is very important to be specific, to know exactly what it is that we are trying to address.

At one of the very first HeadsUp4HTs events in October 2019 Hannah Wilson asked the question 'When did well-being become a thing?', which is an intentionally provocative point. Since then, well-being has increasingly become a feature of daily life, not just in education. Research into well-being is not new, but our focus on it is … so what has changed? The point Hannah was making is that as we increasingly have a sense of an absence of well-being, this is when we start to pay attention to it … but that we shouldn't have to. Surely every human being has a right to *be well*, but the reality is that we find ourselves in a world where this is harder and harder to achieve.

A generative AI search turns up the following results:

> *Well-being is a broad concept that encompasses a person's physical, mental, emotional, and social health factors. It's more than just the absence of disease or illness, and it's strongly linked to happiness and life satisfaction. Well-being can be described as how you feel about yourself and your life.*

Well-being includes:

- quality of life;
- sense of purpose;
- resilience;
- ability to contribute to the world;
- feeling in control;
- experiencing positive emotions;
- perceiving that life's activities are meaningful and worthwhile.

So, we can see that well-being is a multifaceted and dynamic concept that encompasses various aspects of human life. It is often used to describe the quality of an individual's experience and functioning in the world. While its definition can vary depending on cultural, philosophical and contextual factors, well-being generally refers to a state of being comfortable, healthy and happy. This chapter explores the concept of well-being in depth, examining its dimensions, theoretical underpinnings and practical implications.

Defining well-being

At its core, well-being refers to the overall quality of life experienced by an individual. It includes physical health, mental and emotional states, social connections and a sense of purpose or fulfilment. The term is frequently used interchangeably with related concepts such as happiness, life satisfaction and quality of life, although each has distinct nuances. Scholars and practitioners often differentiate between subjective well-being (SWB) and objective well-being (OWB) to capture the complexity of the term.

1. *Subjective well-being* (SWB): SWB refers to an individual's self-reported assessment of their life. It encompasses emotional experiences (e.g. joy, contentment, or stress) and cognitive evaluations of life satisfaction. SWB is often measured through surveys and questionnaires, asking individuals to rate their happiness or satisfaction with life. Factors influencing SWB include personality traits, relationships and daily experiences.
2. *Objective well-being* (OWB): OWB, on the other hand, focuses on external conditions that contribute to a good life. These include access to basic needs such as food, shelter, education and healthcare, as well as broader societal

factors like economic stability, social equality and environmental quality. OWB is often assessed using quantitative indicators like income levels, literacy rates and life expectancy.

Theoretical perspectives on well-being

Well-being has been studied extensively across disciplines such as psychology, philosophy, sociology and economics. Several theoretical frameworks provide insights into its nature and determinants:

1. *hedonic perspective*: rooted in the philosophy of hedonism, this perspective emphasises pleasure and the avoidance of pain as the primary components of well-being. Psychologists like Ed Diener have developed models of SWB (Diener, 1984) that focus on emotional experiences and life satisfaction as central to well-being;
2. *eudaimonic perspective*: this perspective, inspired by Aristotle's concept of eudaimonia, focuses on living a meaningful and virtuous life. It suggests that well-being arises from fulfilling one's potential, pursuing personal growth and contributing to the greater good. Psychologist Carol Ryff's model of psychological well-being (PWB) (Ryff, 1995) aligns with this view, highlighting dimensions such as autonomy, mastery and purpose;
3. *self-determination theory* (SDT): proposed by Edward Deci and Richard Ryan (Deci and Ryan, 2012), SDT identifies three basic psychological needs essential for well-being: autonomy, competence and relatedness. According to SDT, fulfilling these needs fosters intrinsic motivation, personal growth and overall well-being;
4. *capability approach*: developed by economist Amartya Sen (Sen, 1999) and philosopher Martha Nussbaum (Nussbaum, 2000), this framework emphasises the importance of individuals' capabilities – their ability to achieve valuable functionings in life. It shifts the focus from resources and outcomes to the freedoms and opportunities people have to live a good life.

Dimensions of well-being

Well-being is not a singular construct, but comprises multiple interconnected dimensions. These dimensions provide a comprehensive understanding of what it means to thrive:

1. *physical well-being*: physical health is a fundamental component of well-being. It includes factors such as physical fitness, nutrition, sleep and the absence of illness or injury. Regular exercise, a balanced diet and preventive healthcare are essential for maintaining physical well-being;
2. *emotional well-being*: emotional well-being involves the ability to manage emotions, cope with stress and maintain a positive outlook. It includes resilience, self-esteem and emotional intelligence. Practices such as mindfulness, therapy and social support contribute to emotional well-being;
3. *social well-being*: social connections play a vital role in well-being. This dimension encompasses relationships with family, friends and the community, as well as a sense of belonging and social support. Strong social ties are associated with better mental and physical health;
4. *intellectual well-being*: intellectual well-being refers to engaging in mentally stimulating activities and lifelong learning. It involves curiosity, creativity and the pursuit of knowledge. Reading, problem-solving and cultural activities contribute to this dimension;
5. *spiritual well-being*: spiritual well-being pertains to a sense of purpose, meaning and connection to something greater than oneself. It may involve religious practices, meditation, or philosophical reflection. Spirituality provides a framework for understanding life and coping with challenges;
6. *environmental well-being*: this dimension highlights the importance of living in a healthy and sustainable environment. It includes access to clean air, water and green spaces, as well as responsible consumption and environmental stewardship;
7. *economic well-being*: economic stability and financial security are critical for well-being. This dimension involves having sufficient resources to meet basic needs, achieve goals and handle unexpected expenses. Economic well-being also includes job satisfaction and work–life balance.

Factors influencing well-being

Numerous factors influence well-being, ranging from individual traits to societal structures. These factors interact dynamically, shaping the overall quality of life:

1. *genetic and personality traits*: research suggests that genetic predispositions and personality traits, such as optimism and extraversion, significantly affect well-being. While genetics set a baseline, individuals can enhance their well-being through intentional activities and lifestyle choices;

2. *relationships and social support*: positive relationships and strong social networks are critical for emotional and social well-being. Supportive connections buffer stress, provide companionship and enhance life satisfaction;
3. *economic conditions*: economic stability, employment and financial resources directly impact OWB. However, studies indicate that, beyond a certain income level, additional wealth has diminishing returns on happiness;
4. *health and lifestyle*: physical health and lifestyle habits, such as exercise, nutrition and sleep, are closely linked to well-being. Chronic illnesses and unhealthy behaviours can negatively impact quality of life;
5. *cultural and societal factors*: cultural values, societal norms and public policies shape well-being. For example, cultures that prioritise collectivism may emphasise social well-being, while individualistic societies may focus on personal achievement;
6. *life circumstances*: life events, such as marriage, parenthood, or career changes, influence well-being. While people often adapt to changes over time, significant challenges like loss or trauma can have lasting effects.

Measuring well-being

Assessing well-being is a complex task due to its subjective and multidimensional nature. Researchers and policy-makers use various tools and indicators to evaluate well-being at individual and societal levels:

1. *self-report surveys*: surveys like the Satisfaction with Life Scale (SWLS) and the Positive and Negative Affect Schedule (PANAS) measure SWB. Respondents rate their happiness, life satisfaction and emotional experiences;
2. *composite indices*: indices such as the Human Development Index (HDI) and the Social Progress Index (SPI) combine multiple indicators to assess societal well-being. These indices consider factors like health, education and economic conditions;
3. *biomarkers and physiological measures*: biomarkers, such as cortisol levels or heart rate variability, provide objective data on stress and health. These measures complement self-reported well-being;
4. *qualitative methods*: interviews, focus groups and ethnographic studies offer in-depth insights into individuals' experiences and cultural contexts of well-being.

Promoting well-being

Enhancing well-being requires a holistic approach that addresses individual, community and systemic factors. Strategies for promoting well-being include:

1. *public health initiatives*: governments and organisations can implement programmes that promote physical and mental health, such as vaccination campaigns, mental health awareness and fitness programmes;
2. *education and awareness*: schools and workplaces can foster well-being through education on stress management, emotional intelligence and healthy lifestyles. Incorporating mindfulness and social-emotional learning can have lasting benefits;
3. *social policies*: policies that address inequality, provide social safety nets and ensure access to healthcare and education contribute to societal well-being. Examples include universal healthcare and paid parental leave;
4. *community engagement*: building strong communities and encouraging volunteerism and civic participation enhance social well-being. Community programmes create opportunities for connection and support;
5. *personal practices*: individuals can improve their well-being through practices such as gratitude journalling, meditation and regular exercise. Developing hobbies and pursuing meaningful goals also contribute to a fulfilling life.

Challenges and future directions

While significant progress has been made in understanding and promoting well-being, challenges remain. These include addressing global disparities, integrating diverse cultural perspectives and managing the impact of technology and urbanisation. Future research and policy efforts should:

1. *embrace cultural diversity*: well-being is influenced by cultural values and beliefs. Research should explore diverse perspectives and develop culturally sensitive interventions;
2. *leverage technology*: technology offers opportunities for monitoring and enhancing well-being, such as apps for mental health and fitness. However, it also poses risks like digital addiction and social isolation;
3. *address climate change*: environmental degradation and climate change threaten well-being globally. Sustainable practices and policies are essential to ensure a healthy planet for future generations;

4. *focus on equity*: reducing inequalities in health, education and economic opportunities is critical for promoting well-being universally. Policies should prioritise marginalised and vulnerable populations.

Well-being is a comprehensive and dynamic concept that encompasses various dimensions of life. It is shaped by individual characteristics, relationships and societal conditions, reflecting the interplay between subjective experiences and objective realities. Understanding and promoting well-being requires a multidisciplinary and holistic approach, integrating insights from psychology, philosophy, economics and public health. By prioritising well-being at individual and collective levels, we can create a more compassionate, equitable and thriving world.

This is at the heart of the mission of HeadsUp4HTs to create individual and collective approaches to ensuring the well-being of leaders in our education system. We are unable to address all of the aspects of well-being outlined above, but for those that we do have the ability to affect and influence we have created effective strategies. How do we know it works? Our headteachers tell us: of the thousands that we have worked with, 100 per cent of them would recommend our approaches to another leader. While there is inevitably an element of subjectivity in their self-reflections on the impact on their own well-being, that is a statistic that we are immensely proud of. At the end of the day our mission remains focused on the individual – if we can help one headteacher feel better about themselves and their job in any given hour/day/week then our mission is fulfilled.

Case study: coaching support

Since becoming a headteacher four years ago, the challenges have been immense – from staffing to buildings to contractors. The operational side of running a school has, at times, dominated my life, leaving me little time to focus on the reason I am there: the children. It is difficult to summarise the challenges I have faced in just a few words because there are so many. However, one of the biggest for me personally has been leading on my own, without a strong senior leadership team to support me at times.

I feel fortunate that my school has the funds to pay for my coaching and supervision. But what about schools in financial crisis, those struggling with a deficit budget? Headteachers need to know that there are places they can turn to for support without having to worry about the cost.

At one point, I felt I was in a serious crisis. I had no idea what to do or who to turn to as I was the only member of the senior leadership team (SLT) leading the

(Continued)

school during the pandemic. I felt so alone, so isolated – and convinced that I was the worst headteacher in the world, doing a terrible job. I couldn't see a way out of the hole I was in. I cried a lot – in my office, at home – wondering how to carry on.

That was when I found HeadsUp4HTs. It has been amazing! I had a crisis call with James, and later another call with Kate when I was at a particularly low point. I led the school without a deputy headteacher throughout the pandemic, and the challenges were enormous. But HeadsUp4HTs gave me the confidence to lead in such difficult circumstances.

I now attend the Saturday morning meetings and have built an incredible network of people who will support me whenever I need it. I don't feel as alone any more. I have a headteacher 'buddy' who I speak to regularly – we support each other and celebrate each other's achievements.

Through HeadsUp4HTs, I have a place to turn to whenever I need it. There is always someone who will listen, talk and understand. It has helped me realise that I am doing a great job, I do know what I'm doing and I am an authentic leader. I lead with confidence and compassion, and everything I do is for the benefit of the children. HeadsUp4HTs has also shown me that it's OK to cry, to say when I'm not having a good week and to ask for help when I need it.

Headship is lonely. Headship is hard. It drains you, consumes you, and sometimes makes you feel like there must be another path. But it is also the best job in the world. Without proper support, though, many headteachers will burn out. The immense pressures and relentless accountability they face daily are unsustainable. Support must be available to all headteachers.

Because of HeadsUp4HTs, I now have the strength to try things differently, to trust what feels right for my school, my children and my community as we move forward together.

References

Deci, E.L. and Ryan, R.M. (2012) Self-determination theory. *Handbook of Theories of Social Psychology, 1*(20), 416–36.

Diener, E. (1984) Subjective well-being. *Psychological Bulletin, 95*(3), 542–75. https://doi.org/10.1037/0033-2909.95.3.542

Nussbaum, M.C. (2000) *Women and Human Development: The Capabilities Approach* (*Vol. 3*). Cambridge: Cambridge University Press.

Ryff, C.D. (1995) Psychological well-being in adult life. *Current Directions in Psychological Science, 4*, 99–104.

Sen, A. (1999) *Commodities and Capabilities: Amartya Sen*. Oxford: Oxford University Press.

7

The importance of purpose

Maintaining healthy levels of well-being

Purpose is a fundamental component of human existence. It is what drives us, provides direction and lends meaning to our experiences. Whether in the context of personal fulfilment, career aspirations, or social engagement, having a clear sense of purpose is widely recognised as one of the cornerstones of mental and physical well-being. This chapter explores the profound impact that purpose has on our well-being, discussing its relationship with psychological health, physical health and overall life satisfaction. Furthermore, it examines how purpose can be cultivated and how its absence can contribute to mental and physical health challenges.

Purpose has become a fundamental tenet of the approaches we take at HeadsUp4HTs. This is due to the well-researched link between purpose and well-being (see below and Chapter 6). Many of our headteachers will describe their journey towards headship being full of purpose, of wanting to 'make a difference for people'. When we embark on our headship we have a strong sense of connection to this purpose. However, many will describe how that sense of purpose gets lost as the demands of the job, and the demands of the system's requirement of the job, start to erode that connection to purpose. How they find themselves undertaking task after task that feels purposeless. This doesn't necessarily stop them from achieving great things in their school community or the young people in their care having great experiences in their school, it's just that they are unable to see it, swamped as they are by the demands of the job.

By undertaking activity that helps them to recognise and see their success we enable them to make a strong reconnection to their purpose and to find strategies that help them to stay purposeful, while also abandoning some of the activity that becomes a distraction.

> *I have been able to start to value my own worth as a headteacher. It has been wonderful to re-connect with my core purpose. The past few years have led me to question whether this is what I want to do again; this process has helped me to remember just why I made that crazy decision 15 years ago to apply for a headship.*

Defining purpose and well-being

Before delving into the importance of purpose, it is necessary to define what we mean by 'purpose' and 'well-being'.

Purpose is often described as a sense of meaning or direction in life. It is the understanding of one's role in the broader context of life, the motivation to work towards goals and the fulfilment that comes from engaging in meaningful activities. Purpose is a personal and evolving construct that can be shaped by individual values, experiences and aspirations. In short, it provides individuals with a reason to get out of bed in the morning and helps them navigate the complexities of life.

Well-being, on the other hand, is a multidimensional concept that encompasses both subjective and objective aspects of life. Subjective well-being, on the one hand, is typically assessed through measures such as happiness, life satisfaction and positive emotions. Objective well-being, on the other hand, includes factors like physical health, economic stability and social connectedness. Well-being is an integrative state where people feel good emotionally, are healthy physically, have a sense of control over their lives and engage in meaningful relationships and activities.

Purpose and psychological health

Psychological well-being is closely tied to the sense of purpose. In fact, purpose has been shown to be a significant predictor of mental health outcomes. Research has consistently found that people with a strong sense of purpose tend to experience lower levels of depression, anxiety and stress, and are more resilient in the face of adversity. But how exactly does purpose influence mental health?

1. Purpose as a buffer against stress

When we face challenges or periods of uncertainty, having a sense of purpose can help us cope more effectively. A clear purpose provides us with a framework for understanding and responding to stressors. Rather than feeling overwhelmed by difficulties, individuals with a strong sense of purpose are more likely to see them as challenges to be overcome rather than insurmountable obstacles. This shift in perspective can reduce the emotional burden of stress and allow individuals to persevere with greater resilience.

For example, studies have found that older adults who have a sense of purpose are less likely to experience depression and anxiety, even in the face of serious health problems. This is because having purpose provides them with the motivation to continue engaging with life, whether through social connections, hobbies, or contributing to their community. In turn, this engagement reduces the feelings of isolation and helplessness that can lead to depression.

2. Purpose and positive emotions

A sense of purpose is closely associated with the experience of high energy, positive valence emotions, including joy, gratitude and a sense of accomplishment. When we pursue goals that are aligned with our values, mission and passions, we are more likely to experience fulfilment, satisfaction and happiness. These positive emotions, in turn, contribute to greater mental health.

People who have a clear sense of purpose tend to have higher levels of life satisfaction, which is a key component of overall well-being. Life satisfaction is not just about external circumstances, but also about how we interpret our experiences. Those with purpose view their lives as meaningful and coherent, which enhances their overall sense of contentment and psychological flourishing.

3. The connection between purpose and self-transcendence

In psychological terms, self-transcendence refers to the ability to connect with something greater than oneself. Purpose often involves a sense of self-transcendence, where individuals see their lives as part of a larger picture or work towards goals that benefit others. This can provide a deep sense of fulfilment and enrich psychological health.

Studies have shown that self-transcendence, often nurtured by having a clear purpose, is linked to greater psychological well-being. People who focus on serving others, contributing to society, or pursuing spiritual goals often report higher levels of happiness and meaning in life. This sense of connection to others and to something larger than oneself can buffer against existential despair and promote a sense of peace and contentment.

There are too many ways to record the impact of your support in words. I feel connected, listened to and supported. It's been transformational.

Purpose and physical health

While purpose is often discussed in the context of mental and emotional well-being, its influence extends to physical health as well. Research has demonstrated that having a sense of purpose is linked to various health benefits, including improved cardiovascular health, better immune function and increased longevity. In fact, purpose has been shown to be one of the most consistent predictors of physical health outcomes.

1. Purpose and longevity

Numerous studies have explored the relationship between purpose and life expectancy. One of the most compelling findings is that individuals with a clear sense of purpose tend to live longer than those without one. A study published in *JAMA Network Open* in 2020 (Alimujiang et al., 2019) found that older adults who reported a high sense of purpose had a significantly lower risk of death over a 14-year period compared to those with a low sense of purpose.

The exact mechanisms behind this connection are not yet fully understood, but it is believed that purpose influences health through various pathways. For instance, people with a sense of purpose are more likely to engage in healthy behaviours, such as exercising regularly, eating well and avoiding harmful habits like smoking or excessive drinking. Moreover, having a purpose in life can reduce the risk of chronic diseases like hypertension and heart disease, likely due to its positive effects on stress levels, emotional regulation and lifestyle choices.

2. Purpose and immune function

Purpose may also have direct effects on the immune system. Some studies suggest that people with a sense of purpose exhibit stronger immune responses, making them more resilient to illness and infection. One explanation is that the emotional and psychological benefits of purpose – such as lower stress levels and greater life satisfaction – can enhance overall immune function.

For example, research has found that people who score high on measures of purpose show lower levels of inflammation, which is a marker of immune system activation that is often linked to chronic diseases like diabetes, arthritis and heart disease (Guimond et al., 2022). The relationship between purpose and immune function suggests that the benefits of purpose are not just limited to mental health, but have far-reaching effects on physical health as well.

3. Purpose and healthy behaviours

People with a strong sense of purpose are more likely to engage in behaviours that promote physical health. For example, they are more likely to exercise regularly, maintain a balanced diet and get enough sleep – all factors that contribute to longevity and quality of life. Having a sense of purpose may provide the motivation needed to take care of one's body, even in the face of challenges.

In one study, older adults who had a sense of purpose were found to be more likely to engage in physical activity, which is a critical factor in maintaining good health as we age. Additionally, purpose-driven individuals may be more motivated to seek medical care when needed, follow treatment regimens and take preventative health measures (Kim et al., 2020).

> *[HeadsUp4HTs is the] best thing I've joined since being a headteacher; it has encouraged me to stay in the profession, it's made me realise that I need to look after myself so I can be a force of strength for my staff.*

Purpose and life satisfaction

One of the most significant impacts of purpose on well-being is its effect on life satisfaction. Life satisfaction refers to how content individuals are with their lives as a whole. It is a broader measure of well-being that reflects an individual's overall sense of happiness, fulfilment and achievement. Research has consistently shown that people with a strong sense of purpose tend to report higher levels of life satisfaction.

1. Purpose and meaning in life

A key component of life satisfaction is the sense that life is meaningful. People who feel that their lives have a purpose are more likely to view their experiences through the lens of meaning rather than randomness or futility. This perspective can create a profound sense of fulfilment, even when facing difficulties.

A study published *as The Psychology of Purpose* (Adolescent Moral Development Lab, n.d.) found that individuals with a higher sense of purpose reported greater overall satisfaction with their lives, even in the face of adversity. The researchers concluded that purpose helps individuals interpret life events in a way that supports psychological growth and contentment. By framing life's challenges as part of a greater purpose, individuals can maintain a sense of coherence and meaning.

2. Purpose and social connectedness

Purpose often involves connecting with others, whether through work, relationships, or community engagement. These connections are critical to life satisfaction. People who have a sense of purpose tend to have stronger social networks and more supportive relationships, which in turn contribute to greater life satisfaction. The social bonds that stem from shared goals, altruistic endeavours and a sense of shared purpose help to reinforce a person's sense of belonging and contribute to emotional well-being.

For example, studies have shown that people who are involved in volunteer work or community service often report higher levels of life satisfaction. This is because such activities provide a sense of purpose and social connection, both of which are associated with positive mental health outcomes.

3. Purpose and goal achievement

Purpose is also closely linked to the achievement of personal goals. Individuals who have a clear sense of purpose tend to set and pursue goals that are meaningful to them, and the pursuit of these goals contributes to their overall sense of life satisfaction.

Achieving meaningful goals provides a sense of accomplishment and reinforces the belief that life has a purpose.

Furthermore, the process of pursuing a meaningful goal – whether it is related to career, relationships, or personal growth – can foster a sense of progress and self-efficacy. People who feel that they are making progress towards a goal that aligns with their values often experience greater satisfaction with their lives, regardless of the outcome.

> *Through regular support and connection with other new heads, I've rediscovered my sense of purpose and have built the confidence to prioritise my own well-being alongside striving to make a difference in my school community.*

Cultivating purpose: strategies for individuals and communities

Recognising the importance of purpose in well-being raises the question of how individuals and communities can cultivate and sustain it. The following strategies offer practical guidance.

1. Self-reflection and goal-setting

Purpose begins with self-reflection. Individuals can explore their values, passions and long-term aspirations through journalling, meditation, or conversations with trusted mentors. Setting specific, measurable, achievable, relevant and time-bound (SMART) goals provides a roadmap for translating purpose into action.

2. Pursuing meaningful activities

Engaging in activities that align with personal values and interests fosters a sense of purpose. Whether it is pursuing a hobby, volunteering, or advancing a career, meaningful activities provide opportunities for growth and fulfilment.

3. Building supportive relationships

Strong social networks play a vital role in sustaining purpose. Surrounding oneself with supportive, like-minded individuals encourages accountability, inspiration and collaboration. Communities and organisations that promote shared goals and values can amplify the benefits of purposeful living.

4. Embracing lifelong learning

Purpose evolves with life's changing circumstances, and lifelong learning ensures that individuals remain adaptable and engaged. Pursuing new skills, knowledge and experiences keeps the sense of purpose dynamic and relevant.

5. Practising gratitude and mindfulness

Gratitude and mindfulness enhance awareness of the present moment and the positive aspects of life. These practices reinforce a sense of purpose by shifting focus from external pressures to internal fulfilment.

> *The sessions gave us time to reflect. It was comforting to hear of others in similar situations and it helped to build relationships. I feel so connected.*

The broader implications of purpose

Beyond individual well-being, purpose has far-reaching implications for societies and organisations. Purpose-driven communities are more resilient, cohesive and innovative. Organisations that cultivate a sense of purpose among their employees experience higher levels of engagement, productivity and loyalty.

Purpose in education

Integrating purpose into educational curricula fosters holistic development and prepares students for meaningful lives. Programmes that emphasise character education, community service and experiential learning help students connect their academic pursuits to their broader life goals.

Purpose in the workplace

Purpose-driven workplaces prioritise employee well-being and align organisational goals with societal impact. Companies that embrace corporate social responsibility and ethical practices create environments where employees feel valued and inspired.

Purpose in public policy

Policy-makers can promote purpose-driven initiatives by supporting mental health programmes, community development projects and lifelong learning opportunities. These efforts create environments that enable individuals to thrive and contribute meaningfully to society.

Purpose is a cornerstone of well-being, influencing every dimension of human existence. Its psychological, emotional, social and physical benefits underscore its transformative power in enhancing life satisfaction and resilience. By cultivating a sense of purpose, individuals and communities can navigate life's challenges with greater clarity, strength and joy. It is for this reason that purpose is so important to supporting the well-being of school leaders and why we focus so many of our strategies in helping to forge strong links back to purpose.

References

Adolescent Moral Development Lab (n.d.) *The Psychology of Purpose*. Claremont Graduate University for Prosocial Consulting and the John Templeton Foundation. Available here: www.templeton.org/wp-content/uploads/2018/02/Psychology-of-Purpose-FINAL.pdf

Alimujiang, A., Wiensch, A., Boss, J., Fleischer, N.L., Mondul, A.M., McLean, K., Mukherjee, B. and Pearce, C.L. (2019) Association between life purpose and mortality among US adults older than 50 years. *JAMA Network Open, 2*(5), e194270. doi:10.1001/jamanetworkopen.2019.4270

Guimond, A.-J., Shiba, K., Kim, E.S. and Kubzansky, L.D. (2022) Sense of purpose in life and inflammation in healthy older adults: a longitudinal study. *Psychoneuroendocrinology, 141*, 105746. Available here: www.sciencedirect.com/science/article/pii/S0306453022000877 Accessed April 2025.

Kim, E.S, Shiba, K., Boehm, J.K. and Kubzansky, L.D. (2020) Sense of purpose in life and five health behaviours in older adults. *Preventative Medicine, 139*, 106172. doi: 10.1016/j.ypmed.2020.106172

8

A sustainable and intentional approach

HeadsUp4HTs has evolved significantly since its first iteration. During that evolution a couple of words have become really important in regards to the way that we can support school leaders at a system level. They are *sustainability* and *intentionality*.

Sustainability

For us, this means that we provide and share support methodologies that can be sustained by leaders and groups of leaders long after the initial support from the HeadsUp4HTs network has come to an end. Our aim is to create a national self-sustaining well-being support network.

Our reasons for doing this are partly due to the limited resources available. Wouldn't it be lovely to think of each headteacher having access to a coach/mentor/supervisor as and when they needed? The reality is that for 24,000 school leaders this is a multimillion-pound annual commitment and the resources are just not available. Secondary to this is a belief that, as we know with young people in our schools, equipping people with the right tools and skills enables them to have agency and independence in regard to looking after their well-being, individually and collectively. Not only is this much more cost effective, it is arguably also much more impactful in the long term.

In our coaching work, our peer support work and in the creation of our AI GPT application we are intentional about ensuring that the support is sustained long after we have stopped working with a headteacher/group of headteachers. This is achieved as we are able to share a set of actions and strategies that can be tried, adapted and implemented in regular practice by the leader until they become habitual behaviours, practised constantly. These actions and strategies are specifically designed to address the areas that we know leaders are grappling with. Furthermore, in the creation of peer support groups, after we have finished working with the group we train the group members to be facilitators of their own group, helping them to plan how regularly they will meet and providing them with powerful questions to ensure that the group maintains the culture of support and celebration and stays focused on issues related to well-being.

> *However I was feeling when I joined the peer group, I always left feeling more positive, less alone and supported. Allowing myself that hour each week was so beneficial to me, not just as a headteacher, but also as a mum, a daughter and a partner. Our group continues to meet, virtually and in person, and we care about each other. We don't look after each other, but we continue to look out for each other, two years after we all first met.*

Intentionality

It is often the case that support for leaders, especially in the area of well-being, is sought or provided only when the level of stress and anxiety that a leader is experiencing becomes intolerable – that is, the support offer is reactive. Support of any kind is to be celebrated, but this approach has a distinct 'shutting the stable door after the horse has bolted' feel to it. It is the cultural norm in education and is based on an assumption that anyone who has progressed through the leadership tiers must have, and must have demonstrated, high levels of 'resilience'.

The popular 'in tray' exercise employed in headteacher interview processes is both a test of experience/skill and a test of resilience. 'Can this candidate perform under pressure and make good decisions?' is the basis of the activity. In reality the larger majority of leaders in education will have already demonstrated that they are able to do this in the leadership job they currently hold ... in fact education leaders are extremely good at dealing with multiple, varied and complex issues in quick succession in time-limited circumstances. The point here is that education leaders are *very* resilient ... but that all of this rather misses the point!

Of course, education leaders can deal with pressure and the subsequent stress that this might create, this isn't the issue; human beings have evolved a set of psychological and physiological responses to dealing with stress. The point, and therefore the issue for education leaders, is that the responses are designed to protect us in the short term, until the threat has passed; they are not designed to protect us in the long term, for months, or years at a time. This is problematic because education leaders are dealing with limited resources and multiple, varied and complex issues on a daily basis and there is no let up.

Our point is … we know this to be the case. So, we know that headship is both the best and most joyful job in the world *and* incredibly challenging and demanding … and if we know this then let's provide leaders with the support they need – not in a reactive way, but in an intentional and proactive way.

Part of the problem appears to be that the culture in the system resists this notion. The view is binary: we have to either think it is the best job in the world *or* that it is the most challenging. Of course, if you fall into the first camp, there is no issue, everything is going well and why would support be required? If you are in the second camp, you probably thought that you were in the first camp for a significant period of time until the load became unbearable …

So, the first point about intentionality is: 'Let's accept that it is both joyful and challenging and give leaders the tools and support they need at the start of their headship journey and hope that they never need to use them.'

The second point about intentionality is related to research into post-traumatic disorders and how we can recover from traumatic events. In 1995 O'Leary and Ickovics described four possible responses to a traumatic experience (see Figure 8.1 and below).

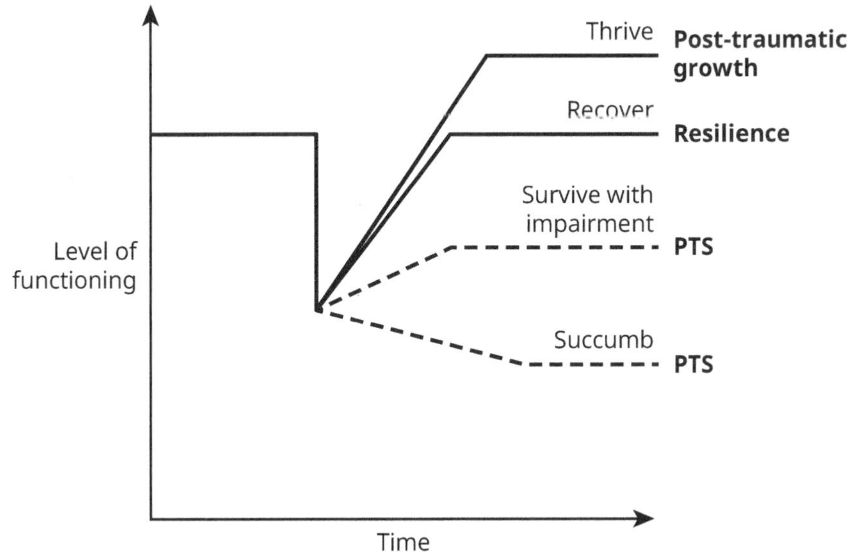

Figure 8.1 Responses to trauma (O'Leary and Ickovics, 1995)

In Figure 8.1 we can see a level of functioning that begins as steady over time. At the point that we experience a traumatic or adverse event our level of functioning drops rapidly (a vertical line downwards). After this, the graph shows four different possible paths for the line to then follow: thrive; recover; survive with impairment; succumb. You will see that with 'thrive', the level of functioning returns to a new stable level above that at the start. With 'recover', the level of functioning returns to that at the start and with 'survive with impairment' and 'succumb' the line levels out at a lower level than at the start.

In their research, O'Leary and Ickovics (1995) categorise four possible outcomes after the trauma:

1. *thrive*: we learn from the traumatic event; we might describe this as *post-traumatic growth*. As a result our level of functioning is, in fact, higher than before we experienced the trauma;
2. *recover*: we are able to use our skills, experience and wisdom to recover from the trauma and return to our pre-trauma level of functioning; we might describe this as *resilience*;
3. *survive with impairment*: in this scenario there is some recovery of functioning; however, we are unable to get back to the level we were at before the trauma. In this scenario we will be suffering with symptoms of post-traumatic stress (PTS or PTSD);
4. *succumb*: in this scenario the trauma is such that we are unable to recover at all and we are unable to function at all; we will be suffering with severe post-traumatic stress (PTS or PTSD).

It is important to state what we mean by a *traumatic* or *adverse* event. The word 'trauma' tends to make us think of a big 'life-changing' event; in reality it can be anything that leaves us with feelings of negativity, either in our ability or in our feelings – for example, a very negative email from a parent could be described as a traumatic or adverse event. Of course, in isolation these traumas or examples of adversity would not lead to post-traumatic stress disorders (PTSD); however, we might find them stressful – that is, we might experience a psychological or physiological reaction. The reality for headteachers and leaders is that they may experience a number of these 'micro' traumas within a short space of time (a day, a week), and it is the collective impact of these over time that may lead to a negative impact on our ability to function and/or PTSD.

The culture in our system that we have described previously – the need for headteachers and leaders to be compelling at all times – means that we might not 'notice' or pay attention to these traumas and their impact; we 'soldier' on without resolving the stressful consequences. Our work with headteachers in crisis reveals that it is often the case that it is the long-term impact of traumas and stress over time that leads them to reach out for support, or indeed be signposted to support by someone in their network. Of course, the fact that support is being sought is to be celebrated, but the reality is that it is a reactive response and too often the fact that the leader has reached crisis means that they have already probably decided that they are incapable of fulfilling the demands of the job. It is in these situations that we see headteachers making decisions to resign from their position, seek early retirement or take a long-term leave of absence.

Our view and experience is that we can be much more intentional about how we help headteachers and leaders to cope with the ongoing and multiple traumatic/adverse events that they will experience in their role. To do this we have to accept that it is 'the best job in the world' *and* 'that it is also incredibly challenging'. If we are intentional, we might provide support at this point (see Figure 8.2).

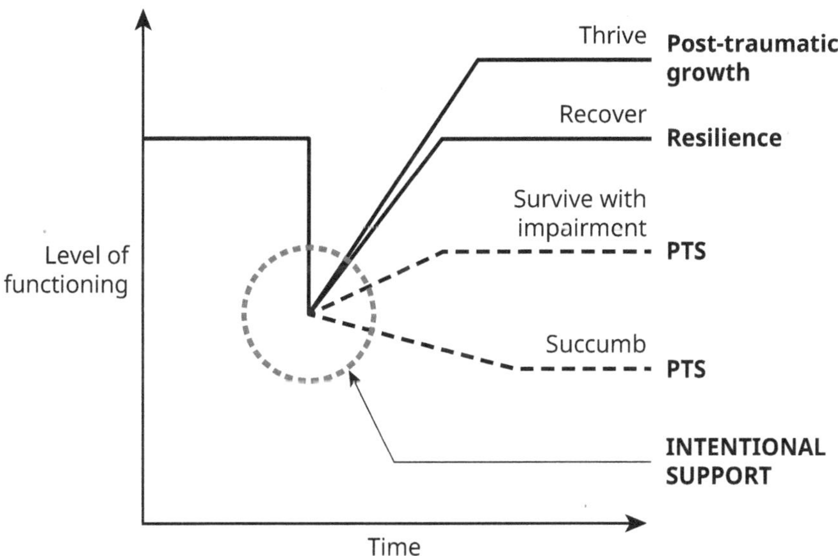

Figure 8.2 Timing of intentional support after a traumatic/adverse event

The intentionality comes because we provide appropriate support to help the headteacher/leader to process the effects of the traumatic/adverse event. In this regard we will likely help them to at least recover and, hopefully, help them to thrive; most importantly, we would hope to prevent them from being impaired or indeed succumbing. It does depend on the access to support being available at the time of the event and, of course, this isn't always possible (for example, if the support is a coaching/mentoring/supervision relationship it may be that the headteacher isn't able to access it for some weeks); it is for this reason that we have developed our HeadsUp4HTs app, so headteachers can access support in real time.

To be intentional in this way requires us to ensure that *all* headteachers and leaders have access to coaching/mentoring/supervision (ideally all three so that they can select the most appropriate version of support to suit their needs). This is not currently the case in our education system and it is why we (and others) do the work that we do and campaign for change in our approaches to supporting our leaders.

It is also the case that while it is better than not doing anything, there is still an element of reactivity to this approach. Therefore, we are also advocates for being intentional at this point (see Figure 8.3).

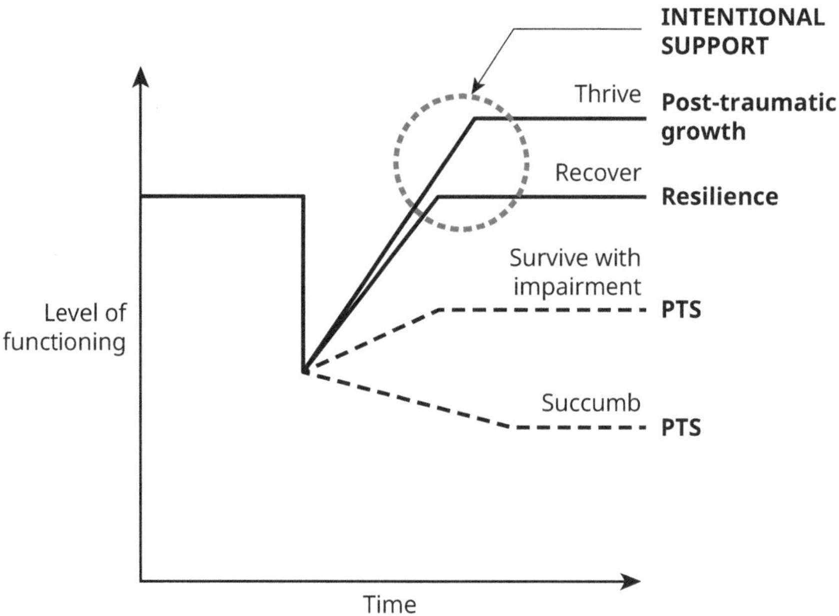

Figure 8.3 Timing of intentional support while a headteacher is at a high level of functioning

In this case, the intentionality is clearly more proactive. We are accepting that the job is challenging and we are providing the headteacher/leader with support *and* tools/strategies/actions that reduce the impact of traumatic/adverse events before they happen. For this to become our systematic approach to supporting leaders we need to achieve two things:

1. *future leaders*: a system whereby headteachers and leaders are provided with support (and the tools to enable them to sustain the support) at the very start of their leadership journey. While we have seen elements of this approach – for example, the government's investment in the early headship coaching offer (EHCO) – too often it is the case that the culture in the system is a barrier to headteachers/leaders acknowledging that the support might be useful;
2. *current leaders*: to ensure that *all* current headteachers/leaders have access to and are encouraged to take up an offer of support and the tools that would enable them to sustain the support irrespective of whether they feel that they are in need of support or not – that is, that they may currently have a high level of functioning, but they recognise that in the future they may experience a severe traumatic event, or a sequence of traumatic events, that may impact negatively on their level of functioning and that to have the support and tools in advance of this happening will be beneficial.

Both cases therefore require a wholesale cultural shift away from the 'hero' leader paradigm of the uber-compelling leader who has no faults or vulnerabilities, towards a culture where we accept that *all* leaders are likely to experience challenges and adversity across their career and that we might be better placed providing them with the tools to address this before they embark on leadership – while they are growing into their leadership role and, most importantly, before they experience the ongoing or severe trauma/adversity that leads them to resign their position.

References

O'Leary, V. and Ickovics, J. (1995) Resilience and thriving in response to challenge: an opportunity for a paradigm shift in women's health. *Women's Health: Research on Gender, Behaviour and Policy, 1*, 121–42.

PART 2

Nine steps to well-being

In Chapter 5 we described the issues that headteachers are facing in regard to their leadership confidence:

1. isolation;
2. impostor syndrome;
3. competition;
4. high-stakes accountability;
5. impact on personal and professional relationships and well-being.

Over the course of the last five years, as we have supported thousands of headteachers to navigate these issues, we have developed what we call our *nine steps to well-being programme:*

1. be honest with yourself;
2. recognise the need;
3. identify the barriers;
4. amplify the things that bring you joy;
5. build a positive self-image;
6. focus on your impact;
7. identify your skills and acknowledge your experience;
8. reconnect with your purpose;
9. nurture connections and build support networks.

In this part of the book we will explore these steps in more detail. We will provide:

1. some context as to why the step is important;
2. practical strategies that you can employ in your working life and beyond;
3. a case study from a headteacher in our network that exemplifies how focusing on this step has supported them with their well-being.

Some of the steps are designed to deal with one of the specific issues, others are more general and help with a number of the issues. It is our intention to share these strategies with you so that you can implement them as and when you need to, building a toolkit for well-being support that will be sustainable throughout your headship. In that regard this is intended to be a highly practical section that you will revisit time and time again.

Which steps you decide to focus on will very much depend on which of the issues is particularly relevant to you at this moment in time. We are clear that not all of the strategies will work for you; a little like exercising to maintain physical well-being, it is up to you to discover what works for you and what doesn't. Similarly, as with exercise, these strategies are unlikely to work if implemented for short periods of time. While there will be an impact, it will not be sustained, so wherever possible try to make these strategies part of your working life, to be regularly practised and to enable you to be consistent in what serves you. To aid this, most of the strategies are very simple and require little time. It is not our job to add to your workload! Rather, we provide you with the tools for you to create your own well-being toolbox.

As described in Chapter 8 it is also the case that these practices are helpful regardless of where you are on the joyful–challenged spectrum (see Chapter 3). Our approach is designed to be intentional. These practices are as much about maintaining healthy levels of well-being as they are about repairing a low level of well-being.

To aid the ongoing sustainability of your practice we recommend that you start a leadership well-being journal. This will be a place for reflection, but also, over time, it will be a source of positivity when you are experiencing a dip in your personal leadership rollercoaster. As educators we love any excuse to secure ourselves a lovely piece of stationery, and if you would like your journal to be specifically focused on our practice then please do look out for our HeadUp4HTs journal which is a companion to this book.

If you are particularly tech-enabled then you may find that our HeadsUp4Hts app is a useful alternative to the journal (see Chapter 18).

9

Step 1: Be honest with yourself

'How are you?'

When we ask the question 'How are you?' at HeadsUp4HTs, we *mean* it. It is often, but not always, the case that headteachers rarely get asked this question, and if they do it is often in passing or as a forerunner to a meeting. The phrase has become a polite, but somewhat meaningless exchange; yet the truthful answer – and the courage and vulnerability involved in it – is the starting point for raising greater self-awareness and well-being.

How you are is fundamental to the successful operation and strategic development of your school. In the early days we would say: 'If we get the head's head right, then everything else has a far greater chance of success.' Therefore, this is a fundamental step in the well-being journey for leaders. As described in Part 1, there is a balance to be maintained between being seen and perceived to be a compelling leader by everyone in our communities and being honest about vulnerabilities and inner fears regarding our capacity and capability to be a headteacher.

We want to be perceived to be compelling ... 'I've got this' ... and therefore this is the persona we present to all of those around us. We have to work hard to maintain the compelling persona. If someone asks us 'How are you?' (which may be rare), it is unlikely, if we are feeling vulnerable, anxious or stressed, that we are going to tell the questioner the honest answer. As a consequence, we become adept at creating a series of deflective responses:

- I'm OK;
- I'm alright;
- I'm good;
- I'm fine, how are *you*?

These deflective responses are not in themselves the issue; it is entirely possible that it would not be appropriate for you to share your fears and woes with the person asking. We call the tendency to maintain this external projection to all of those around us the *cloak of invincibility*.

The issue arises when we start to tell ourselves that we are OK, alright, good or fine, when in our heart of hearts we are not and we know we are not. When we are not being honest with ourselves, when we wear the cloak of invincibility constantly, we create a damaging internal conflict ... and a narrative of personal mistrust. We know we are not OK, but we persuade ourselves that we are; in the course of this internal dialogue we create a scenario where our self-esteem is further damaged because we berate ourselves for not meeting the expectations that we have set for ourselves. We learn to ignore the signs that our well-being is being negatively affected and 'just get on with it'. As a consequence, we do not change our behaviours or take any proactive actions to address the feeling.

I'm OK, I'll just keep going.

Our ability to be honest with ourselves is further impacted by the culture in the system. Think about the times that you come together with other leaders – local authority meetings, headteachers' conferences – it is often the case that in these spaces our need to be perceived as really compelling is heightened further. We make assumptions that everyone else is confident, competent and knows more than we do. We fear speaking out or speaking up in case we look foolish or incompetent.

Of course, everyone in these spaces is doing the same thing that you are doing, so we create an environment whereby everyone is showing themselves off to be their best, even if internally they don't feel like that, and this further contributes to developing a culture where we are not able to be honest about how we are truly feeling about our role. This can be toxic and contributes to an environment whereby we do not feel psychologically safe. (It also feeds the inner critic/impostor syndrome which we discussed in Chapter 5.)

The following point is important, but can be difficult to get across without implying criticism: this local culture grows as a consequence of the system culture that has been created around the high-stakes accountability environment in which we exist. An example of this is seen when James is presenting on well-being. He will occasionally find that some leaders think it is important to share how much they love and enjoy their job; they can sometimes be quite angry and confrontational about making this point. Of course, the fact that they are loving and enjoying their job is to be celebrated, see Part 1, but, in their public stating of this fact to a room of other headteachers, some of whom might not be feeling so positive, they immediately shut down the possibility for those who are struggling to share that feeling with others for fear that it demonstrates weakness and/or failure. Much of our behaviour in this regard is unintentional, but the point here is that we are responsible for the culture we create and if we are to build intentionality into our approaches to leader well-being we have to accept that the job is both joyful and challenging (the power of *and*, see Chapter 8).

> *Staying vulnerable is a risk we have to take if we want to experience connection.*
>
> (Brown, 2022, p. 102)

On the flip side it is also the case, and this point is just as important, that we rarely notice when we are feeling really good about ourselves. It is rightly our expectation that we should be feeling good, therefore we don't notice it and appreciate it. Consequently, the times when we are feeling negative are the times that resonate with us. This then becomes the narrative that builds around our headship; we create a self-fulfilling prophecy where we only remember the negative moments and feel how challenging the job is. So, a) 'It's OK to not be OK', as long as you take appropriate action, and, b) if you are feeling OK let's recognise it: 'I am OK'.

The strategies outlined below are useful in both scenarios, helping us to take action to improve our sense of well-being and enabling us to sustain it in the longer term. Relevant issues being addressed with these strategies are: isolation, impostor syndrome, competition, high-stake accountability, personal and professional relationships.

Step 1 Strategies to employ

Ask yourself 'How are you?'

You should respond with a one-word answer, but you are not allowed to use the deflective responses outlined above (reminder: OK, good, alright, fine). This is much more challenging than you might think, so take your time to think of your one word. Once you have your word, unpack it further by reflecting on the meaning that word has for you at this moment in time. Then ask yourself why you are feeling this way.

1. Try to establish this practice into your working diary

It is a short activity and does not require a lot of your time. The more regularly you can build this into your working day the better chance you have of capturing those moments when you are feeling very positive about your role.

2. Start to keep a journal as a record

Do you notice any patterns? Are there certain times of the day when you are likely to feel more positive or negative? Why is that? Are there certain activities that you are undertaking that help you to feel more positive or negative? (See later strategy regarding diary management which extends this activity further.)

3. Create a time to discuss how you are with someone else in the organisation

It is likely that this might be your chair of governors or a line manager in your trust. If you don't feel safe being vulnerable with someone you work directly with, then you may benefit from a non-judgemental and supportive space like the HeadsUp4Ts peer support sessions. Over time you may become comfortable enough to have this conversation with someone on your senior team (if you are lucky enough to have one). This is not an admission of failure; it is much better for this to become a regular feature of your conversations in an open and transparent way than for them to find out that you are struggling to the point that you can't cope further down the line!

4. Create openness and transparency across your senior team

Over time, regular conversation based around the 'How are you?' question helps to create a shift in culture whereby we become more purposeful and intentional in regard to well-being among our staff.

Case study: Dan's journey

The power of honest leadership

Dan Nixon, Mount Pleasant Church of England Junior School

Before I began coaching, my professional and personal lives felt completely incompatible. It was exhausting. I convinced myself things were fine, masking how I really felt to maintain composure. At work, I'd answer 'I'm fine' to staff or colleagues, even when I wasn't. I felt stuck in a cycle that didn't seem sustainable.

Coaching changed that. It gave me a safe space to reflect and be honest, both with myself and others. One of the first shifts was recognising how meaningless 'I'm fine' had become. Coaching pushed me to pause and really answer the question, 'How are you?' – not just for the sake of saying it, but to figure out what I could do about it. If I wasn't fine, what steps could I take to make things better?

I started being more intentional about my responses. Instead of the automatic 'fine', I might say, 'Actually, I'm having a good day' or 'It's been a tough one'. It felt awkward at first, but I quickly realised the power of honesty. When I shared openly, others followed. Staff began to share their struggles in a constructive way, and conversations became more meaningful. It shifted the culture in our school. Honesty became a strength, helping us move past surface-level interactions to build trust and deeper relationships.

I also realised that being honest with myself wasn't just about words – it was about action. If I checked in and recognised I wasn't OK, I would take steps to address it. I started proactively planning work-from-home days, unapologetically creating space to prepare or recover. I embraced the importance of balance. I've encouraged my team to do the same, and it's been transformative.

Through this journey, I've also embraced vulnerability. I've always been open about my own mental health challenges. Coaching with Kate helped me see vulnerability as a leadership strength. By sharing my experiences honestly, I've created an environment where staff feel safe to open up – whether it's about personal challenges or frustrations with work. Nothing's off the table.

Of course, I've had to find the right balance. Early on, I sometimes shared too much, which could overwhelm others. I've since learnt to be appropriately honest, expressing how I feel without overloading those around me. That balance has been key to building stronger, more supportive relationships.

(Continued)

For me, answering 'How are you?' authentically has been transformational. It's not just about the words – it's about what comes next. Being honest with myself has helped me lead with integrity, create space for others and build a more sustainable way of working. My advice? Stop saying you're fine when you're not. Reflect, take action and don't apologise for prioritising your own well-being.

Dan's recommendations:

- continue to be honest with yourself about how you are feeling and proactively manage your time and energy levels;
- encourage staff to be open and honest about their struggles, and create a safe space for these conversations;
- ensure robust systems and processes are in place in the school so that you can step away when needed without the school operations being affected.

Reference

Brown, B. (2022) *The Gifts of Imperfection: Let Go of Who You Think You're Supposed to Be and Embrace Who You Are*. London: Simon & Schuster.

10

Step 2: Recognise the need

'Why is it important to look after yourself?'

As discussed earlier in this book, all of the headteachers in the HeadsUp4HTs network have a common purpose derived from their motivation as teachers; broadly, we are here to make a difference for other people. School leadership is therefore an *act of service to others*. It is a common philosophy of all those who work in schools. As teachers and support staff we want to see young people develop and become successful young adults; as leaders we want the same *and* we want the adults in our community to be successful too.

We therefore have a tendency to go out of our way to support and help others in our communities. It is the reason why the day that we have planned can often get disrupted. We want to respond and react to resolving a problem or issue that has arisen for someone else in our community. It is both a part of the joy of the job and also a reason why it can be so challenging. We will often find that our own workload gets pushed to the side in order to support and help others. Our tendency to be fully available, accessible and reactive to school life due to our empathetic and service-oriented leadership styles, often means that our strategic work – the work we are often held accountable for as leaders – is infiltrated, pushed aside in favour of being supportive in the moment. If this is happening frequently, then it can lead to frustration and overwhelm at not being 'strategic enough', as we are constantly reacting to the needs of the school community.

We are able to recognise in the moment and in the longer term that this has an impact on both how we manage our own workload and our own energy levels. Headteachers are extraordinarily good at managing this complexity; they tend to be super-efficient and effective, in regard to their own workload. Furthermore, we develop a series of adaptations and skills that enable us to operate in this way. (I'm sure you can remember a time when you weren't a headteacher and you would look at your headteacher and ask 'How do they do that?')

Some of the adaptations we make to our own working practice can be damaging in the longer term, and therefore detrimental to our own well-being (e.g. pushing our own work into evenings and weekends, finding that we have less time to be strategic). We can even create a false narrative around these adaptations and working behaviours, that it is 'just the job'. In this narrative we become increasingly reactive. The key point here is that you are not indestructible and you are not a superhero, no matter how good you are at your job! You are a human being before you are a headteacher.

The reality for most headteachers is that they know they should be looking after themselves better, but the inclination to serve others overtakes them. We therefore need to be conscious in our decisions and efforts to look after ourselves ... and to do that we need to recognise the higher need: self-care isn't selfish!

When we are able to do this then we are able to better meet the needs of school leadership in the longer term. By explicitly recognising what we implicitly understand and then taking action we not only ensure that we can be amazing leaders for years to come, but also we become a better role model for those that might be thinking of following in our footsteps.

To give ourselves permission to do this can be very hard as it can feel that it is in direct conflict with our purpose. If this is the case for you, then it might be necessary to seek that permission from elsewhere, such as school governors. (One of our partners is the NGA; we believe governors have an important role to play here.) This is where this step builds on step 1 – by having an honest conversation with our governors about 'how you are' we can then take intentional steps towards identifying the appropriate investment in support for you.

Ultimately, if you are struggling to give yourself permission, at least recognise the following:

- you can't pour from an empty cup;
- it is important to put your own oxygen mask on first;
- it is in the long-term interests of your employer and the school community that you lead that you look after yourself;
- if you look after yourself, you are in a better position to look after/out for others and to be the best leader you can be.

Relevant issues being addressed with these strategies: isolation, personal and professional relationships.

Step 2 Strategies to employ

You need to set boundaries to enable you to thrive.

1. Identify your needs

As a school leader, start by asking yourself: 'What do I need to thrive in my role?' Reflect on what supports your well-being, productivity and sense of value. Consider your physical and mental health needs, such as adequate sleep, time to think strategically and time for personal reflection. These are crucial for your ability to lead effectively and remain well.

2. Set boundaries to protect your needs

Once you've identified your needs, set clear boundaries to protect them. For example, if you need sleep to function at your best, ensure that you set a reasonable time to wind down each evening, avoiding work after a certain hour. If you need time for strategic thinking, block off dedicated periods during the week where you can work without interruptions. Establishing boundaries like these helps you maintain the energy and clarity required for effective leadership.

3. Communicate your boundaries

Clearly communicate the boundaries you've set to your staff. Let them know why these boundaries are important for your well-being and for your effectiveness as a leader. Be transparent about your need for reflection, meetings and strategic planning. Encourage your staff to respect these boundaries and remind them that it's essential to model healthy practices for the entire school community.

4. Reflect and commit to positive change

Regularly reflect on how your boundaries are supporting your well-being and leadership. Are you getting enough sleep? Are you managing time to think strategically? If something isn't working, change it! Encourage your staff to engage in similar reflection and create an ongoing conversation about the importance of boundary-setting. Boundaries aren't hard and fast rules, they can be changed to suit your own needs and energy.

Breaking a downward spiral in school leadership

A downward spiral can begin with overwhelming challenges like staffing issues, financial stress, or isolation, which can lead to negative self-talk and a feeling of helplessness. This mindset often intensifies the perception of failure, causing school leaders to lose perspective and confidence.

To escape a downward spiral, consider these three steps.

1. Reframe negative thoughts

Pause and challenge catastrophic thinking. Ask yourself: 'What is the likelihood of this worst-case scenario happening?' or 'Is this the most realistic outcome of the situation?' This helps to shift focus from fear to a more rational and constructive mindset.

2. Confide in a trusted colleague or friend

Share your concerns with someone you trust. Talking openly can provide relief, reduce isolation and allow you to gain support and practical advice from someone who understands your challenges.

3. Gain perspective

Step back and consider the bigger picture. Focus on solutions by asking: 'What can I realistically control or influence in this situation?' Perspective helps you approach problems with clarity and resilience.

Rest, relax, rejuvenate

Leaders are used to planning their working days, weeks and terms, but less intentional about planning their time away from work. The way we spend our time and energy away from work also supports the way we spend time and energy in work. Resting, relaxing and rejuvenating are all necessary to supporting our well-being. Each one is different, and each one is different to each of us. It's important to be intentional about all three, particularly in the school holidays, but, essentially, throughout the school term too. Again, this is about maintaining a sense of well-being and thriving as a leader, as opposed to just surviving term by term.

Case study: Liz's journey – recognising the need

Liz Harros, Executive Headteacher, East Riding Local Authority

Two years ago, I was utterly burnt out and broken on the inside, but from the outside, my colleagues saw me as some kind of superwoman. They would say, 'I don't know how you do it.' The truth was, I wasn't doing it – not really. As an executive headteacher managing three small schools, the pressures were overwhelming. I was spinning multiple plates, from strategic responsibilities to serving school lunches. The workload was unrelenting, and the demands of OFSTED were brutal. During one traumatic inspection, I snapped. I walked out of the school while the inspection was still underway, convinced I'd never return to the profession.

That experience left me traumatised – something I later recognised as akin to PTSD. I withdrew from colleagues, avoided meetings and disconnected from any form of support. Isolated and filled with self-doubt, I couldn't see a way forward. It wasn't until a trusted colleague expressed genuine concern for my well-being that I realised I couldn't carry on like this. Even so, reaching out for help felt like an act of courage.

My first step towards recovery was signing up for a BootCamp with HeadsUp4HTs. I was hesitant and sceptical. In hindsight I wasn't ready for it, but it turned out to be the transformative point in my journey. I even remember telling another headteacher there, 'I don't understand why coaching makes such a difference to you.' She replied, 'I don't understand why it doesn't.' That moment stayed with me. Now, I understand why it makes a difference. Now, I get it.

I subsequently signed up for coaching with HeadsUp4HTs funded by my local authority. The early sessions were raw and painful. Letting someone into the world I'd carefully shut others out from was difficult, but it was also necessary. One pivotal moment came when my coach noticed how my face changed when I spoke about the children. That observation helped me reconnect with my purpose, my ikigai, *and I remember the joy that had drawn me to education in the first place. Slowly, I began to strip back the resentment, hurt and exhaustion, and rebuild a sense of self-worth.*

The process wasn't just about rediscovering my purpose; it was also about recognising the importance of self-care. Basic things like eating, sleeping and journalling became acts of restoration. I started to see that self-care wasn't selfish, it was essential for me to lead effectively and authentically.

(Continued)

Headship is a rollercoaster, with constant ups and downs throughout the term. What coaching and the HeadsUp4HTs community gave me was a sense of balance – something to steady me amid the chaos. Meeting with other head-teachers regularly provided a safe space to share experiences, gain perspective and feel heard. It wasn't a 'pity party', but a place for authentic connection. That connection smoothed out the rollercoaster ride and helped me maintain resilience.

Accepting that I needed support was the hardest step. Yet today, I lead with clarity and confidence, and I accept that I have wisdom to share through my experiences and vulnerability and that connecting with others is essential to me thriving in my role.

Liz's recommendations:

- you are the priority – your health and well-being matter;
- don't wait until you're at breaking point to seek help. Coaching and connection aren't just for times of crisis – they're vital for maintaining balance and perspective;
- take the leap, be open to support and you'll find it can change everything.

11

Step 3: Identify the barriers

'What's stopping you from thriving?'

Once we have reflected on how we are and ascertained that it is vitally important that you look after yourself, we then have to identify what it is that is stopping us. After all it is probably the case that, at a deeper level, you already understand these things, all we have done in steps 1 and 2 is make the implicit explicit!

When we ask headteachers in the HeadsUp4HTs network what the barrier is to them looking after themselves it ordinarily boils down to one of three things:

1. time;
2. resources;
3. self-limiting beliefs.

Time

It goes without saying that headteachers have plenty to do. The to-do list can seem never-ending and it evolves constantly to include those things that you have planned to do and those things that are bound to happen in a complex human organisation where individuals have free-will, minds of their own and don't necessarily always behave in the way we might want them to. It therefore goes without saying that time is precious and it is inevitable that many headteachers struggle to find the time to focus on their well-being in the busy environment of their school. Of course, the work of a headteacher is not just confined to the hours of a school day; they will often find themselves working late into the evening at home, which in itself doubles the impact as it detracts from time we might otherwise spend pursuing those things that help us to rest, relax and rejuvenate and/or with loved ones, family members and friends ... the very things which might help us to replenish our reserves and help us with our well-being.

If time is the barrier, then there are things that can be done to address that (see below).

However, we also suggest that time might not be the barrier; rather it might be our energy levels. If our well-being is low then it is likely that our energy levels are low also (and vice versa) – the to-do list tackled in September is probably approached with a different level of energy to a similar to-do list in November! We are not as effective when our well-being is low and we are feeling tired and exhausted. Consequently, the demands on our time go up as tasks take longer than they should.

So, our priority here is to focus on maintaining higher levels of energy and mitigating against the energy-sapping consequences of the emotional high and lows of headship, taking the rollercoaster and smoothing it out a little!

Resources

We have already established that headteachers are likely to spend a lot of their time concerned with the well-being of others before themselves. It therefore is to be expected that in a world of limited resources we prioritise those resources towards something that helps others before we would ourselves. Specialist coaching/mentoring/supervision support for leaders is a long-term investment. There are two issues here:

1. *permission* (see above): we would argue that the decision to spend money on this type of specialist support should not be left in the hands of the very leader who might perceive it as being extravagantly selfish (even if there is a long-term benefit to the community in a headteacher who is maintaining a high level of well-being) and governors/trusts have a role to play here;
2. *cost*: even with permission it may well be that the necessary funding cannot be found. We accept that this is the case and it is why sustainability is at the heart of the HeadsUp4HTs peer support model (and our app). It is through effective peer support networks that we can build low-cost and impactful well-being support to leaders.

Self-limiting beliefs

Often a barrier to looking after ourselves and therefore thriving comes from the assumptions we make about ourselves, what the role should 'look like' and what other people think of us. Headteachers will often articulate a sense of guilt around investing in themselves, especially if there is a financial/resource cost or an impact on the time we can devote to the role (see above). When we coach around the 'guilt' narrative, we get to the essence – it's a fear of being judged.

While these three barriers are significant it is also the case for many of our headteachers that they haven't given their own well-being enough thought and consideration. Therefore we might describe one of the barriers as careless negligence; after all, behaviours are established over a long period of time. Just as when we put weight on, it is not because we have had one high-calorie meal, but that we have been eating too many calories over a long period of time ... we don't notice we have put weight on in the moment – we notice it some time later when suddenly that favourite item of clothing is feeling a little too tight! Similarly, we might adapt our behaviour when it comes to our workload to cope with short-term stress and then find that what we thought might be short term has suddenly become a long-term adaptation to ongoing heightened levels of stress. We've been so busy adapting and dealing with what is in front of us we have neglected to take care of ourselves.

Relevant issue(s) being addressed with these strategies: isolation, personal and professional relationships.

Step 3 strategies to employ

Reflection: what's stopping you thrive?

The next time you feel that you are thriving, take a moment to pause and reflect. What are the conditions? When you are not thriving, what is stopping you, what is getting in the way?

- When are you most productive?
- When are you most able to give your full attention to tasks?
- Try planning your working day around your energy levels – for example, if you're a high-energy morning person, then is it better to tackle any meetings and difficult conversations in the morning?

(Continued)

- If your energy levels dip in the afternoon, why not ensure the office door is shut for an hour and address some less emotionally demanding and forward-facing tasks such as replying to emails.
- Tracking your energy levels throughout the day can help with noticing patterns and forward planning your operational and strategic tasks throughout the school day.

1. Conversation with governors

Regular discussion about what support would be most useful and how the barriers to accessing this support can be overcome.

2. Diary management

We have included this strategy here; in reality it is useful across a number of the steps and connects into other strategies too. The basis for this strategy is to take proactive action in regard to the activities that fill our diaries. It is a three-stage activity.

a. Over a period of two weeks evaluate each activity in your diary through the lens of energy. Colour code each activity:
   i. *green – energy giver*: this is an activity that you were looking forward to and during the activity you felt joyful. Afterwards you felt uplifted and energised (NB these activities are likely to have a strong alignment to your sense of purpose, see later);
   ii. *red – energy drainer*: you were apprehensive or anxious about this activity before and during. Afterwards you felt negative and de-energised (NB these activities are likely to feel purposeless, see later);
   iii. *amber – energy neutral*: neither of the above.

b. After two weeks, group the different activities together by colour coding in your leadership well-being journal. What patterns are there? What types of activity energise you? What types drain you?

c. As you plan your diary moving forward, colour code the activity on the basis of your evaluation. Be mindful of any days with a high number of red activities:
   i. can you fit some green activity in on this day to achieve a sense of balance?
   ii. if not, be mindful about how you might feel at the end of the day and be kind to yourself.

Additional strategies to try based on this activity.

a. Always try to end the day with a green activity; you will take this energy home with you and will have a sense of positivity which will impact your evening.
b. Always try to end the week with a green activity; you will take this energy home with you and it will likely impact your whole weekend in a positive way.

3. Downloading

This strategy is especially useful if you find that your sleep is being disrupted by the mental load of your work. It is likely, if you have been struggling with sleep, that you have tried well-established strategies such as having a notepad and pen by your bed for when you wake up in the night. However, we often hear from HTs that this doesn't work for them, this is often because the 'job' is so present and important to us that a part of our mind is always devoted and working on it. Not only can this disrupt our sleep, but it can often mean that we are not present in our personal life. Practising downloading can help with both of these issues.

a. Before you leave work to go home make a note of all of the things that you are thinking about that are 'present' and at the forefront of your mind. Capture them in a planner or notebook. The practice of writing them down is the first step in downloading or decluttering our busy minds.
b. Repeat this activity at the point in your evening prior to when you properly sit down to relax, when any home-based jobs/chores and/or any work you needed to complete at home have been finished.
c. Repeat the activity just before you go to bed.

The act of repeating this activity two to three times over the course of an evening has two outcomes:

a. by downloading and decluttering our conscious mind of the things we are thinking about in a defined way and allocated period of time we have a better chance of being present and of having restful and peaceful sleep;
b. the emptying of our conscious mind is more likely to stimulate our subconscious mind and 'shake loose' those things that we were not even aware that we were thinking about; it is likely that these are the things that we wake up thinking about in the middle of the night.

If it appears that time and resources are insurmountable barriers to us thriving then the strategies identified in steps 4–9 will assist with this as many are low-demand, quick activities.

Case study: Kate Smith, HeadsUp4HTs network leader and coach

As a well-being coach, I have had thousands of conversations with incredible headteachers. My role is to help them identify the barriers that hold them back – from becoming the leaders they aspire to be and from prioritising their own well-being. Time and again, I see dedicated leaders wrestling with unspoken, self-imposed barriers that stop them from leading authentically and taking care of themselves.

Headteachers work within a high-stakes accountability system that fosters a culture of constant availability and perceived omnipresence. This culture isn't only driven by external pressures; it is also internalised through narratives shaped by past experiences, observations and expectations. Many headteachers began their careers under leaders who operated in very different circumstances – leaders whose approaches wouldn't align with the demands of today's educational landscape. Additionally, our own perceptions of headteachers from our school days often reinforce outdated ideals, fuelling unrealistic comparisons and feelings of impostor syndrome.

These inherited narratives create a critical inner voice that whispers: 'I can't leave before 6pm', 'I'll do the strategic work in my own time', or 'there will be a safeguarding incident if I work from home'. Justifications like these often conceal deeper drivers: fear of judgement and the heavy weight of accountability.

Fear manifests in many ways for headteachers: fear of being seen as less committed if they work from home; fear that delegating tasks might overburden staff, leading to burnout; fear that stepping back might invite criticism in a profession constantly under scrutiny. These fears often become silent decision-makers, leaving little room for leaders to reflect on what truly supports their well-being or aligns with their values.

While accountability is essential, it can become oppressive when paired with such fears. The belief that effective leadership requires personal sacrifice often crumbles when unpacked in a coaching session.

Leaders who refuse to check emails at night do not become ineffective.

Headteachers who prioritise working from home occasionally do not lose their staff's respect or invite operational failures.

These realisations, though liberating, can also feel destabilising, as they challenge long-held beliefs.

Permission offers an antidote to this fear-driven narrative. It begins with the courage to ask: What do I need to thrive? What kind of leader do I want to be? These simple, but profound questions open the door to a leadership style rooted in alignment with values.

Granting yourself permission is not indulgence – it is courage in action, and it is transformative. It means embracing discomfort and saying, 'This is what I need to lead authentically'. It is a recognition that well-being is not a luxury, but the foundation of sustainable leadership.

As a headteacher, waiting for permission to lead in a way that feels right can hold you back. Instead, consider the power of granting yourself that permission. This act of self-leadership is transformative, reinforcing the importance of prioritising well-being – not as an afterthought, but as the foundation for leading with energy, authenticity and sustainability.

Kate's recommendations:

- if you are doing your best with the resources you've got, then don't beat yourself up;
- create boundaries to ensure your own needs are met; thriving leaders know the importance of prioritising their own well-being in order to lead well in their schools;
- you are only ever responsible for your own happiness. You are not responsible for the happiness of others, only they are. Do your best to create conditions where staff and children can thrive.

12

Step 4: Amplify the things that bring you joy

'What brings you joy?'

We started the job with joy, didn't we? (see Chapter 3). The things that resonate as joyful, in both our personal and professional lives, do so because they are hardwired back to a sense of purpose (Chapter 7). Due to the demands in our workloads, however, we can often miss these joyful moments while we spend our time focused on those things that are not working well in our school and responding to the external factors that are demanded of us. So, we can spend much of our time focused on those things that are not inherently joyful, and if there is any joy to be found in them it is likely that it is going to come much further down the line once change has been delivered ... by then we will have moved on to the next thing to be improved, and on it goes!

Sadly, we are working in a system where often school accountability is disguised as school improvement; we are forced from above to constantly focus on what's wrong and not yet good enough in our schools. The reality for most schools is that while there are always things that need changing, the majority of what is happening in your school is great! Children are in classrooms learning and laughing, staff are developing and reflecting, environments are uplifting! We can't rely on our school improvement systems to focus on what is joyful and positive about our schools; rather we have to take responsibility for ourselves. Ask yourself not what needs improving, but: where are the gems in your school? What's great about it? How do we amplify it? Replicate it? Share it with others?

For all of us there will be special activities that we undertake – maybe echoing back to our time in the classroom – that feel precious to us. We may have initially been good at ring-fencing time devoted to these special activities and perhaps, over time, the demands of the job have been such that we stopped doing them, we broke the habit.

The basic principle here is that if we find an activity personally joyful then the likely reason is that it feels purposeful. If it feels purposeful it is almost certainly contributing in some way to our sense of well-being. Therefore: a) be more present in those moments and b) plan more of those things into your working day.

Engaging in activities that bring you joy provides an immediate boost to your well-being. However, there's also a more subtle, secondary benefit connected to step 4: you're likely to be reminded of the positive impact you're making in your community.

Relevant issues being addressed with these strategies: impostor syndrome, personal and professional relationships

Step 4 Strategies to employ

Reflection: all the things that bring you joy

1. Write a list in your journal of all of the things you do in your personal and professional life that bring you joy. Take your time and ensure that you include things that you might not have done for a while. For each thing on your list identify:
    a. how does it feel when you do that thing?
    b. when was the last time you undertook that activity?
    c. the last time you participated in the activity were you truly present? If yes, great; if not, why not?
2. In your diary for the next week identify times when you can participate in those activities, diarise those moments and commit to doing them in the same way you would a meeting. Try to fit one into every day that you are in school.
3. At the end of each activity reflect on how you feel, ask yourself 'How are you?'
4. At the end of the week reflect on how you feel, ask yourself 'How are you?'

1. Planning the joy in school leadership

Joy doesn't always just happen – it can be intentionally planned, especially in the demanding role of school leadership. By embedding joy into the school culture, leaders can create a positive environment that uplifts staff and enhances their sense of purpose.

2. Take time to notice the good stuff

Schedule moments to step away from your office and walk around the school, not to observe or assess, but simply to notice what's going well. This time should be agenda-free, focused on appreciating the small, but significant moments: a teacher engaging a class with enthusiasm, a child proudly sharing their work, or the buzz of a collaborative activity. Scheduling time for staff to do the same can help them see the bigger picture and reconnect with the purpose and joy of their roles.

3. Plan time for connection and celebration

Joy can be contagious. Building in time for staff to come together and share successes fosters a sense of community and boosts morale. This could be as simple as a short meeting where staff highlight something that has gone well that week or a dedicated slot during INSET days to celebrate collective achievements. Even when individual leaders may struggle to see joy themselves, hearing others' positive experiences can reignite a sense of shared purpose and pride.

4. Model joy as a leader

As a leader, your actions set the tone. Make a habit of noticing and acknowledging good things in your interactions with staff and students. Whether it's a thank you for a job well done or simply pausing to celebrate small wins, these actions ripple through the school, building a culture of appreciation and positivity.

Planning the joy is not an indulgence; it's a vital part of creating a school culture that thrives. When leaders and staff take time to celebrate, connect and focus on the positives, they build resilience, motivation and a shared sense of purpose – essential ingredients for successful happy schools.

Case study: Kirstie's journey – finding joy in leadership

Kirstie Willis, Head of School, Briar Hill Infant School

As a school leader, my journey has reinforced the profound importance of finding joy in the role, even amid its many challenges. Reflecting on this, I've always been a 'silver lining' person – someone who actively seeks the good, even when things don't go as planned. Life is full of challenges, and resilience, paired with joy, is key to navigating them.

Joining HeadsUp sessions during the COVID-19 pandemic was a turning point. At a time when school leaders felt isolated and overwhelmed, the sessions with Kate became a lifeline. Initially, I was apprehensive, as I'm naturally quite reserved, but the warmth and support from the group were transformative. We shared diverse experiences, yet we were united by a common goal: to give our children, families and staff team the very best support. A seemingly simple question posed during those session – 'How are you?' – became a cornerstone of my leadership. When asked sincerely, it creates space for meaningful dialogue and shows people they are truly heard. That sense of authenticity and care has been instrumental in how I behave and lead.

Leadership isn't about projecting constant optimism, alluding that everything is perfect or dismissing others' concerns. It's about authenticity; acknowledging when things go wrong, embracing the lessons and finding ways to move forward. For me, joy is deeply tied to building a culture of appreciation. Whether it's saying 'thank you' at the right moment, celebrating a colleague's efforts, sharing how grateful you are for the team around you; these acts amplify positivity and strengthen our team. For instance, recognising our RE lead for her incredible work on the new curriculum, well-supported and appreciated by the teaching team, not only celebrated her achievements, but also reinforced our collective sense of purpose and teamwork –layers of appreciation.

Feedback has also become a significant part of our school's culture. Once met with hesitancy, feedback is now welcomed as a tool for growth and connection. It's a way of saying, 'I value you, and I want to help you thrive'. When things go well, we share that joy openly, creating a ripple effect of gratitude and motivation. When challenges arise, we address them constructively, within a no-blame culture, knowing that resilience and support are part of our foundation.

Joy, for me, is not fleeting or superficial – it's an intentional act of recognising the good in any situation. I see it in the small, but significant moments: reframing a challenging morning for a colleague, helping a child reset their day, always taking time to walk the school each day to witness joy in action within our school community. These moments remind me why I love what I do and the impact of taking time to share joy can have on others.

Staff well-being is a priority. Every meeting starts with an activity focused on joy, whether it's reflecting on positive contributions or playing lighthearted games. These rituals aren't frivolous – they create a culture of connection and shared purpose. Teachers spend so much time at school, often more than with their families during term time, so it's crucial that the environment feels safe, supportive and authentic.

Ultimately, finding joy is about balance. It's about recognising the challenges, but choosing to amplify the good. By shifting the focus from 'what's going wrong' to 'what's going well', I've been able to lead with purpose and inspire the same in others. For me, joy is about collective success, shared gratitude and the small, meaningful moments that remind us why we chose this path.

Kirstie's recommendations:

- intentionally plan joyful activities with your team, in order to have things to look forward to and things to celebrate – capturing as much of this as you can;
- have perspective and lead by example; develop a culture where finding the joyful moments is natural for all and an embedded part of the daily routine – this is especially important on challenging times;
- joyful moments are happening in school all the time; make sure you give yourself time to walk your school daily to see them and celebrate them – the ripple effect is that this brings joy to you, to the children and to your team.

13

Step 5: Build a positive self-image

'Who are you at your best?'

We have already discussed the overtly negative culture that pervades the education system. Despite all of the evidence to the contrary, it can sometimes feel as if we are not doing a very good job. Our schools are constantly portrayed as failing their community in some way or another, even if they are judged to be doing a good job by our harshest critics. It is also the case that it can feel that we are constantly being asked to do more in an environment that has considerably fewer resources than it has had in the past. Furthermore, a larger part of the work undertaken by head-teachers can fall into problem-solving; some days can feel like a never-ending series of fires to be extinguished, leaving us emotionally drained and devoid of energy.

Consequently, a large majority of our feedback loops provide us with negative information:

- a poor behaviour incident is evidence that all behaviour is poor or getting worse;
- a negative email from a parent can feel like all parents are unhappy;
- a difficult situation with a staff member can leave us feeling that all staff are against us.

While it is almost certainly the case that lots of what is happening in our schools is positive and very good, as school leaders we are submerged in a world where we are dealing with the things that might not be.

These feedback loops can feel unrelenting; as we put one fire out another one ignites. This feeling will be amplified if we are not feeling 'at the top of our game', we are tired or overwhelmed and our well-being is low.

No wonder then that it can sometimes feel that we are not capable or do not have the capacity to do the job and be a headteacher. It is within this world that we can doubt ourselves and allow an internal narrative to take hold, building a negative self-image. Whether we feel this occasionally or constantly it is useful to have something to counter it.

The idea behind building a positive self-image is to have a visualisation in our minds of what we look like, who we are and how we behave and feel – on our best days. The visualisation becomes a reminder on the more negative days that we have not landed in the position we are in by chance, that we have a set of values, characteristics and attributes that we have developed and honed over a long period of time (also skills and experience, but we will deal with those in step 7).

We have a tendency to notice when we are not at our best because those moments are discomforting and discombobulating. They tend to stand out and therefore we remember them. The majority of time, while we might not be at our best, we are still doing a pretty good job; indeed, there are moments in any day or in any week when we will get into a *flow state* – we are on top of everything, the to-do list has been tackled with vigour and energy, every problem brought to our door is dealt with decisively and with a smile on our face. We walk the school with a spring in our step and everything feels right with the world.

We feel confident.

We feel competent.

We are in flow.

The aim of this step is to notice when things are going well, both in the moment and reflectively – to reinforce the notion that we have both the capacity and the capabilities required to be an excellent headteacher and to do our job well. The aim is to create a positive self-image and the factors that give us strength, so that we can draw on them when we need to ... also to recognise the circumstances and conditions in which that positive feeling flourishes. If we can identify the conditions in which we find ourselves in a flow state then we can try to replicate them at other moments, thus taking us from a reactive state to one where we can be proactive.

These activities raise a deeper awareness of who you are and what you do well as a leader.

Relevant issues being addressed with these strategies: impostor syndrome, competition, high-stake accountability.

Step 5 strategies to employ

1. Draw an outline image of yourself (if you are building your leadership journal do it on a page in there). Start off by identifying and focusing on the visual characteristics. The easiest way to undertake this activity is to imagine you were going to interview for a new job – what would you wear, what would you look like, ideally how much sleep would you have got the night before, what would you have eaten for your breakfast? Write these things around your outline. Undertake a values exercise (if you already have, brilliant!). Identify your core values and add them to your diagram roughly where your heart would be. Be honest and authentic; this is for your eyes only!
2. Identify your character strengths. www.viacharacter.org has a quick and accurate free-to-access way to do this. Add your top five strengths to your diagram where your head is.
3. When you next find yourself in a flow state pause and take notice. The aim here is to identify the conditions; be quite detailed: how much sleep did you get last night? What did you eat for breakfast? What did you drink? What time did you leave for work? What was the journey like? What did you listen to on the way? What was it like when you arrived at school? What was the first thing you did when you got to work? What was the first task you undertook? Where are you sitting in your office? What does your diary look like for the day? What is the mix of activities that you have (i.e. the balance between things you enjoy doing and things that you don't)? What activity were you undertaking when you noticed you were in flow? Etc. … (you get the idea). What you will have collected is a series of conditions that have probably contributed to you feeling great. Not all of them will be relevant, but why not collect them all. Add them to your diagram around the outside (it would be interesting to compare some of them to the list in step 1).
4. Start to think about how you can recreate those conditions on another day … Can you engineer your flow state? Give it a go and reflectively cross-reference to your self-image in your journal. As you continue to notice new things add them to your diagram.

Who you are and what you do

It's easy to default to introducing yourself by your job title: 'Hi, I'm Kate, a head-teacher.' But you are so much more than your job description! When was the last time you took the time to reflect on *who you are and what you do* as a leader? This isn't about defining your impact for OFSTED, your local authority, or others – it's about defining *your* personal narrative.

What's the story you tell others about yourself? More importantly, what's the story you tell yourself? Start by writing a reflective personal statement – not for your next headship application, but for you. Begin by getting clear on *who you are* – your values, your passions – and what truly matters to you. Then consider *what you do*: the impact you make, the aspects of your leadership that align with your core values and the practices that bring you purpose and pride.

Refine this into a single paragraph. Imagine being out in the hot seat and being asked to introduce yourself as a leader in one minute. Create a clear, authentic statement about *who you are and what you do* as a leader. By grounding yourself in this personal truth, you'll create a positive self-image that reflects your unique strengths and values, reminding yourself – and others – that you are so much more than a job title.

14

Step 6: Focus on your impact

'How do you recognise and celebrate your achievements?'

This is very much linked to the culture of negativity that pervades our education system, as previously described. The consequence of this culture is that school leaders are driven to spend all of their time focused on the future and what needs to be 'fixed' next; we might view this as the *improvement agenda*. While this is right and proper (although we would prefer to use a term which is slightly less loaded with negativity – such as development rather than improvement), it means that there is rarely any time to reflect and focus on the impact that we have already had. If we spend all of our time focused on what needs to be done next and never spend any time reflecting on what we have already done then the danger is that we find ourselves in a state of perpetual and relentless doing/fixing ... which is exhausting and can lead us to think that we are not having any impact at all.

On the rare occasions that we do reflect it is nearly always through the lens of the school/organisation, for example:

1. gathering evidence for our self-evaluation form;
2. analysing results in the summer.

In both of these cases the purpose of the activity is to identify what needs to be done next; if there is any moment of celebration it is often the case that it is fleeting. This is particularly stark when it comes to exam results analysis. Rarely do we spend much more than minimal time or energy reflecting on all of those children who have been successful as a result of the hard work and dedication of staff in the school; rather we are immediately drawn to those children that didn't do as well as we would have wanted and from this we spring into action to address those deficits for the next cohort.

The second issue here is that the reflection is focused on the school/organisation, it's not a personal reflection of impact. This isn't all that surprising; leaders have a tendency towards modesty – when we do celebrate it is nearly always the case that we are doing so on behalf of other people in our organisation. Again, this is not problematic, in fact it is a real strength of school leaders that they do this; however, if we never spend any time reflecting on *our own* impact then there is a real danger that we begin to create an internal dialogue where we don't think we are having any. No wonder then that many of the leaders we have worked with describe a sense that they are failing in their role when in reality the absolute opposite is true.

The third issue is that a significant proportion of a school leader's time is spent creating a culture in which others (young people and staff) can flourish. In this work it is likely that we are doing less of the doing and therefore it can be much harder to find concrete examples of an action that we have taken which has directly led to something changing or developing. Again, even if this is the case it is often that we have done this through others and therefore we celebrate their work rather than recognising our own role in this. In creating the vision and then developing the culture and strategies in which this vision can come into focus for everyone in the community, much of our work and influence can be hard to define and, in lots of cases, goes entirely unseen.

These strategies and actions are therefore very much focused on you and your impact. By noticing and keeping a personal record of our impact, we create an alternative and positive narrative over time (long term) that balances any specific moments (short term) we may have where we feel that we are not doing a very good job and that we are not having any impact at all. We call this strategy inspirational moments (some of our HTs call the activity their positive affirmation walks (PAWs)) and, like step 5, this helps with our self-image and acts as a counter to the sense of impostor syndrome. It can also highlight and amplify the positive reality of life in our schools as a counter to the more negative narrative that tends to beset our education system. The reality is that our schools, as places of human activity and relationships, are filled with inspirational moments every single day. However, because most of us are focused on what needs to be improved these moments pass us by, unnoticed

Relevant issues being addressed with these strategies: impostor syndrome, competition, high-stakes accountability, personal and professional relationships.

Step 6 strategies to employ

1. *Inspirational moments.* The basis for this activity is very simple, but it is very powerful. Take five to ten minutes to walk around your school (or part of your school). Your aim here is to notice those things that put a smile on your face. This may be something quite specific related to a strategy that you have implemented or it might be something more vague, related to the vision, values and culture that you have created. The key here is it doesn't need to be something *big* (it might be as simple as seeing a child open a door for another child or member of staff). When you get back to your office make a brief note of each inspirational moment (start a section in your journal of inspirational moments – leave quite a few pages, you will start to build quite a list!). (Expand on this activity around purpose in step 8.)
2. *Inspirational walks.* Start to diarise an inspirational moment walk every day to build a habit of looking for the impact that you have had on the school community. It is important to keep these walks separate from other moments when you are walking around your school so that your focus is solely on looking for impact.
3. *Share your inspirational moments with others* (staff, SLT, governors, family members). This is the start of creating a culture where everyone notices a positive impact. In this regard there are three results: a) impact on you, by communicating these moments you are reinforcing the positive effect; b) people around you start to see you talking positively about what has been done and this impacts on them; c) it encourages those around you to do the same (see below). (NB Leaders we have worked with have found that this activity can have a profound effect on their personal relationships.) It is often the case when someone asks us how our day has gone that we inevitably focus on those things that have been challenging or difficult. Over time this can build a concern or a worry in them that the role is always challenging and difficult, and obviously because these people love us it can lead to a misrepresentation of the balance between joy/challenge, which leads them to become concerned for us and our welfare. This is an entirely unintended consequence; however, many of our HTs will articulate this. So when someone in our personal life asks us how our day was ... sharing an inspirational moment with them instead shifts the dial on the narrative, imparting something of the joy of the job.

4. *Make inspirational moments part of the culture of your school.* This is a great activity to kick off meetings (with governors, SLT and staff); it only takes five minutes, but can shift everyone's thinking away from deficit into something more positive; it is a salient reminder before we deal with the agenda that, as a team, we are having an impact in our community. Ask people in the meeting to pair up and share an inspirational moment from the last week; you will see a noticeable shift in people's demeanour in this activity as it is impossible to share an inspirational moment without smiling.

15

Step 7: Identify your skills and acknowledge your experience

'Face and embrace your impostor syndrome.'

Working alongside steps 5 and 6 this is a continuation of personal and positive affirmation. The reality is that all headteachers have become headteachers as part of a process of personal development and success over a lengthy period of time; in this regard we have 'earnt our spurs'. In this journey we will have spent plenty of time reflecting on the skills and experiences we have acquired in each of our different roles. When we apply for the next step, we reflect deeply on these things as part of a role application and interview process (this doesn't necessarily feel comfortable, but it is a requirement so therefore we do it!). Then we become a headteacher and suddenly it can feel like everything that went before is irrelevant, that we are being 'judged' against a different set of criteria, a different benchmark. Couple this with our inner vulnerability and tendency for us to be judged in the moment, at any given moment in our headship, and it's no wonder that we can start to doubt that we have the skills and experience to do the job.

Again, the opposite is true; during our journey to headship we have acquired all sorts of diverse skills and experiences. We are drawing on this skill set and these experiences constantly in our daily working life, making decisions and taking action in an almost subconscious way. Because it is subconscious it is easy for us to overlook the skills and experiences we are utilising. And, our skills are often and easily challenged (in a world of excessive judgement); rarely do we have the opportunity to reflect upon them. Of course, appraisal is an opportunity for us to do this, but again we often spend more time thinking about our areas for development than we do thinking about our skill set.

Step 7 Strategies to employ

1. Write a list of the skills you have acquired throughout your career (as a teacher, as a leader and if you have had an alternative previous career from that as well). This will not feel easy at first; try to think through the many aspects of your role and/or look at your diary for the previous two to three weeks, specifically at each concrete activity. For each one think about the skills you had to employ in that activity. Use your diagram from step 5 (or produce a separate one).
2. Over a period of a few weeks keep revisiting this list and add any things that you might have missed.
3. Highlight on your list any skills or areas of skill where you think you are particularly experienced. You might find it useful to write down any particular experiences you have had in your career that feel particularly formative.
4. Spend some time reflecting on your list. You will probably notice a number of things; it is likely that two of them will be: a) your skillset is vast and b) it is highly varied.
5. Try to make this reflective activity a regular feature of your year (termly/annually) as you will be acquiring new skills and experiences and extending your current skill set constantly.

Case study: Overcoming impostor syndrome as a young headteacher

Anonymous

Becoming a headteacher at just 31 years old was a proud moment for me, but it came with a unique set of challenges. As one of the youngest leaders in my area – and a 'dad teacher' with a young family of my own – I often felt the weight of self-doubt creeping in. While I was confident in my abilities to lead students and staff, I couldn't shake the feeling that others might see me as inexperienced or not professional enough. These doubts were especially loud in forward-facing environments, like when speaking to parents. I'd think, 'Do they trust me to lead their children?' or 'Do they think I'm too young for this?'

The impostor syndrome didn't affect every aspect of my role. In fact, I thrived on working with the team, solving problems and being in the heart of the school. But as soon as I had to address a room full of parents, the anxiety hit. My inner critic would shout: 'You're not strong enough' or 'You don't belong here'. One particular parents' evening stands out. Despite having prepared thoroughly, I couldn't shake the feeling that I didn't measure up. It was then I realised I had to address these thoughts before they held me back.

The first step was self-awareness. I spent time reflecting and recognised that my fears weren't rooted in reality, but in perception. My age and experience as a young father weren't weaknesses; they were strengths, offering a unique perspective and relatability to parents. But knowing this wasn't enough – I needed practical ways to change my thinking.

I sought support through coaching, specifically in public speaking and leadership. My coach helped me reframe my self-doubt and encouraged me to identify my strengths. Around the same time, I connected with a mentor, an experienced headteacher, who reassured me that impostor syndrome is common, especially for young leaders. Hearing their journey was inspiring and reminded me that these feelings didn't define my abilities.

I also started practising in low-threat environments. I'd test ideas in smaller meetings, speak to smaller groups of parents informally and gradually built up to larger audiences. These opportunities helped me prove to myself that I could connect and lead effectively. The more I practised, the less intimidating those forward-facing moments became.

The biggest breakthrough, though, was learning to listen to positive feedback. For years, I'd dismissed kind words as politeness, while giving far too much weight to my inner critic. Slowly, I learnt to internalise the compliments I received. Parents appreciated my authenticity and approachability, and those comments began to outweigh my fears. I also reminded myself that no one expects perfection – they value genuine care and leadership.

Over time, I've grown more confident. Public speaking no longer feels like an ordeal, but an opportunity to connect with the school community. Looking back, I'm proud of how I turned self-doubt into strength. Today, I use my experience to encourage other young leaders, showing them that impostor syndrome is something you can overcome – with self-awareness, support and practice.

16

Step 8: Reconnect with your purpose

'What's your why?'

It is always the case that when a leader becomes a headteacher they do it with intent and determination. This is true even in cases where a senior leader steps into the role of headship due to unforeseen circumstances. Alongside the development of leadership skills as we progress through our leadership journey we also experience increased clarity around how we think a school should operate and our educational ideology comes more sharply into focus. At the point at which we become a headteacher we have a strong sense of purpose (see Chapter 7).

A strong connection to our purpose … or our *why* is fundamental to a sense of well-being. If it feels to us, at a deep and fundamental level, that the work we are doing is purposeful then it is highly likely that we will have a very positive sense of well-being, even if we feel overworked and exhausted!

A connection to purpose underpins many of the strategies shared in steps 1–7; however, it is here in step 8 that we start to pull all of that together, taking the practices that we have developed and the daily actions that we can take to support our well-being and drawing them together to maximise the impact on our well-being in the longer term.

Step 8 Strategies to employ

Whether you are feeling joyful about your job or if you are feeling that you are in a particularly challenging moment, this reflective activity is a great way of helping you to discover or rediscover a sense of purpose.

None of us are where we are without a continuity and connection to the decisions and action of our past; we are a narrative built around a lifetime. In this activity you are going to reflect on your narrative. It is a written activity and therefore a great one to put at the start of your leadership journal.

Refection: Why am I a headteacher?

The aim of the activity is to answer the question 'Why am I a headteacher?' To answer the question, you will likely need to reflect on your career and the moments in your career that led you to be in the position that you are in. An additional staging question to help you tell the story is 'Why did I become a teacher?' (or 'What brought me into education?'). This is important as the reason why you became a headteacher will be fundamentally linked to the reasons why you became a teacher and/or why you enjoy being a teacher. To answer the supplementary question it is highly likely that you will need to reflect on your own education and the career path you decided upon.

It is not necessary to overthink your narrative – you are not writing an autobiography for publication! Just settle down to write it (or use some tech to dictate it and take some of the heavy lifting out of the job).

As you write it you will come across important and decisive moments in your life – we call these hinge points – moments where your life could have taken more than one direction, but you chose the path that has led you to where you are today. (If you have seen the movie *Sliding Doors* ...) When you encounter one of these moments in your narrative, pause and reflect and, in parentheses, write: Why did I make this decision? And how did I feel? When you reach the end of your narrative collect all of the bracketed statements together ... you are likely to find some commonality in both the 'why' responses and the feelings. They will be strongly linked to your sense of purpose. Try to distil them down into one statement.

The process outlined above is beneficial in a few ways: a) if you have become disconnected from your purpose it is a great way to reconnect; b) if you already have a strong sense and understanding of your purpose it is highly affirming to see it present in your life's work; c) as you write your narrative out you will get a strong sense of positivity from the impact that you have had across your career.

Additionally, this is an excellent activity for leadership teams to do with each other – although this should be handled with care; it can be a very emotive process and takes careful facilitation. Contact support@headsup4hts.co.uk if you would like to know more about this.

Inspirational moments

In step 6, focus on your impact, we introduced the idea of inspirational moments. These work in the present because they help us to focus on the positive impact that we have had and are having in our community. Additionally, it is highly likely that the things that put a smile on our face and give us a sense of positivity, as seen in our community, will be hardwired back to our sense of purpose. If you take a look at your list of inspirational moments you will probably see this shine through very clearly. This is exemplified when we do inspirational moments activities with large groups of educators; it is always the case that someone's inspirational moment will involve another human being and something that they did or achieved. It is never the case that someone shares something related to the more functional or operational aspects of working in or leading in a school. That is not to say that these things are not important (although see abandonment below), it's just that they do always seem obviously purposeful.

Ikigai

This Japanese philosophy is a fundamental part of our approach at HeadsUp4HTs. *Ikigai* broadly translates as 'your reason for being'.

As you can see, Figure 16.1 is a Venn diagram with numerous points of cross-over … and at the heart is your *ikigai*, your reason for being, or your purpose.

We think the diagram is pretty self-explanatory, but here are some notes to guide you:

- start with 'What I'm good at?' You can draw from the activities in steps 5–7 here;
- next write a list of the things that you love about your job, try not to be too high-level about this – be detailed;
- you will almost certainly find lots of cross-overs between your list of things that you are good at and the things you love … these things are your passion;
- instead of 'What the world needs', look at 'What your community needs' – write a list;
- the cross-over between the things you love and the things your community needs from you is your *mission*.

Now we assume that you are getting paid for the work that you do! So, we don't focus on that section here (although it is super useful if you are looking at a career change!).

Figure 16.1 Finding your *ikigai*

Therefore, your profession is fairly obvious, but it is worth spending some time reflecting on the *vocation* section … this should be the intersection between what you are being paid to do and what your community needs from you; you might want to evaluate how much of a cross-over there is here. For example, how much of the work that you do that you are being paid for is truly focused on what the community needs from you? Which leads nicely into …

Abandonment

We first came across the idea of abandonment as described by the wonderful Sir David Crossley. David makes the point that we are excellent at adding things into our schools as a result of new initiatives, but that we are less intentional and clear about abandoning the previous activity that the new activity has been designed to replace.

In our version we use the idea of purpose as an incisive tool to remove things from the headteacher to-do list. It is always the case that there are lots of things on the to-do list – some of them urgent, some of them in the medium to longer term. The way we approach these activities and the energy we bring to them will often be related to how purposeful we think the activity is; on the basis of the thousands of conversations we have had with HTs it is highly likely that there are some things on the to-do list that sit there for a long time ... they almost certainly feel purposeless. Other activities will instinctively feel purposeful and we are likely to approach these with a real sense of positivity.

Look at each item on the list and ask yourself the simple question 'Why – what purpose does this serve?' If it is not immediately obvious that there is a strong link back to your sense of purpose or the school purpose then you should reflect on whether this thing can be abandoned *or* whether you need to rethink the purpose and therefore rethink the activity. A worked example:

> *school self-evaluation form* (SEF): this nearly always comes up as an item of deep frustration for headteachers. It feels like a huge job and can sit on the to-do list for lengthy periods of time. Whenever we talk about this and ask why they are doing it the answer nearly always comes back to OFSTED. Now it is a long time since OFSTED had any requirement for schools to complete a self-evaluation form/document. What they do want is a clear sense that you have a deep understanding of the strengths and areas for development of your school. Regardless of this point OFSTED is not a strong enough reason to produce an SEF; there has to be a better purpose. So, possible outcomes:
>
> 1. you cannot identify a clear purpose for producing one, so you stop – abandonment (as long as you are confident, you, and other leaders, can demonstrate that deep understanding in some other way – see below);
> 2. you decide that there is a clear purpose for producing a SEF and you continue to do so. However, your self-reflection will have subtly altered the way you approach it; because you have decided there is a purpose for it beyond OFSTED you will feel more positive about completing it;
> 3. you decide that self-evaluation is important and purposeful, but it doesn't necessarily need to be in the form of a document, so you reimagine and redefine the self-evaluation processes and the systems that support it.

It is often the case that, when we look at the to-do list with the scalpel of purpose, 1. or 3. are the outcomes – that is, we stop doing something ... which frees up time and energy for other more purposeful activity *or* we reimagine the activity with purpose and therefore we create a more joyful replacement for the task that is preying on our minds.

17

Step 9: Nurture connections and build support networks

'You are not alone.'

Isolation is one of the five issues that headteachers will always reference as having a negative impact on their well-being. Headship (and leadership generally) is a contradiction in regards to this. We are surrounded by people all day every day; however, we have this sense of isolation that comes with the decision-making authority and the accountability agenda – the things that we don't think we can share with anyone, even our closest confidantes. It is these things that can leave us feeling isolated and lonely.

The activities outlined above undertaken for ourselves, but then shared with colleagues and other headteachers, will almost certainly help to reduce your sense of isolation and loneliness (this is the basis for our peer support model, where we work with groups of headteachers. If this is of interest to you then please do contact us on support@headsup4hts.co.uk).

Nurturing connections and building support networks will almost certainly reduce this further and provide you with virtual and physical spaces where you can share the load of the job in a psychologically safe environment.

Step 9 Strategies to employ

Strategies for connecting with communities and networks.

1. Network mapping

Reflect on the full scope of your professional and personal networks by creating a visual map. Write your name in the centre of a page and surround it with the names of individuals and organisations in your current and past networks. Consider whether any dormant connections could be rekindled for mutual benefit.

2. Assess give-and-take relationships

For each connection, evaluate what you give and receive. Are they acting as a coach, mentor, champion, or nourisher? Ideally, relationships should involve mutual support. If you notice one-sided dynamics where you give more than you receive, reflect on whether those connections serve your needs.

3. Evaluate and balance your network

Analyse your network to identify where you are receiving support:

- as a headteacher and school leader;
- for your personal well-being as an individual;
- for inspiration and passion in education.

If support is concentrated in one area (e.g. leadership), explore new connections to strengthen your well-being and passion for the profession.

4. Join HeadsUp4HTs

Building intentional connections with like-minded, values-driven headteachers is vital for personal and professional well-being. You should by now have a strong sense of what we have created for school leaders at HeadsUp4HTs. We provide an empowering network of school leaders who embrace courage in vulnerability and prioritise mutual support. Engaging with our community ensures you have a safe space to share challenges, celebrate successes and grow, both emotionally and professionally.

By intentionally connecting with a network whose mission is to support you in being the best leader you can be, you'll strengthen your emotional resilience, enhance your well-being and rediscover your passion for leadership.

Case study: The power of networks and connections – Northumberland LA peer group

Headteachers often face immense responsibilities that leave them feeling isolated and overwhelmed. For one group of school leaders, joining a HeadsUp4HTs peer support network funded by Northumberland County Council transformed their experience of headship. What began as a group of strangers evolved into a thriving community of colleagues, friends and champions, offering vital support through the highs and lows of leadership.

When the group first met, the headteachers spanned a range of experience – some were new to the area, while others had been in Northumberland for decades. Despite their differences, many faced similar struggles. As one headteacher reflected, 'I didn't have anyone I could be completely honest with – there was no space to be vulnerable without fear of judgement.'

One headteacher, who was new to the local authority, described her early experience:

> I literally didn't know a single person. I felt really lonely and isolated, and I also felt like I always had to know the answers. It was not OK to not know what I was doing.

Another headteacher, who had been in the area for years, shared similar feelings despite her extensive experience:

> Even though I'd been in Northumberland a long time, I didn't feel I had a group where I could talk honestly and be vulnerable. Schools were in competition, and with OFSTED's pressures, you couldn't say, 'My school isn't doing great,' or, 'I'm not doing great.' It just wasn't the culture.

The personal toll of headship was also a significant shared challenge.

> Work followed me everywhere. I was trying to unpick and unwind at home, but doing it alone. It was unhealthy and was taking too much of a toll.

These shared feelings created a natural foundation for connection. From the first meeting, the group offered a safe space where the headteachers could speak openly without fear of judgement. As one headteacher expressed, 'From the first meeting, I felt an enormous sense of relief. I hadn't realised how much I needed it.'

(Continued)

The openness of the group was underpinned by trust and a commitment to authenticity. Headteachers described taking off their masks and receiving unconditional support. 'It only works because everyone is all in – there's no holding back.' A key outcome of the group was its profound impact on well-being. The headteachers rediscovered the importance of setting boundaries and making time for themselves. They adopted the idea of 'pink things' – joyful activities that nourish the soul.

> We started celebrating moments outside of school – beach walks, family time, hobbies. It reminded us that we're more than just headteachers.

The network also helped headteachers redefine their relationship with work.

> It's OK to say, 'Today's been enough.' I don't feel guilty for not working all night. It's made me a better leader and allowed me to sustain a job I love.

For many, the group offered a space to process work-related stress:

> I've stopped trying to explain the job to people who don't get it. My time with friends and family is now quality time because this group gives me the space to process work.

This positive shift extended to their teams. Headteachers modelled healthier behaviours, inspiring their staff to do the same. 'I leave early two nights a week, and my staff see me doing it. They've started following my example, looking after themselves too,' said one headteacher.

Beyond personal well-being, the group strengthened the headteachers' leadership and advocacy. The trust within the network gave headteachers the courage to take risks, challenge systemic pressures and push for change. One headteacher explained:

> When you know you've got a group of people backing you, it's easier to speak up and stand firm on what's right for your school.

The group also served as a source of immediate, practical support. The headteachers highlighted the power of the WhatsApp group they created following on from the coach-led sessions:

> At any point, you can just say something, and someone will come back with support. You're never waiting days or months – it's instant reassurance.

Since the group began two years ago, there have been meals out, secret Santas, school visits and hours of online weekly catch-ups and self-sustaining support sessions. The group's journey from isolation to connection demonstrates the transformative power of a HeadsUp4HTs supportive network. By sharing openly, prioritising well-being, committing to supporting each other, the group – who were once strangers who shared a job title – created not just a professional community, but more ... a circle of trust and friendship that sustains them through the challenges of headship.

The group's recommendations:

- *be open and honest*: don't be afraid to share how you're really feeling; when everyone's honest, it creates trust and makes the group work;
- *look after yourself*: a support group helps you realise it's OK to set boundaries and make time for yourself; you'll be better for it – and so will your school;
- *learn from each other*: there's so much to gain from hearing others' experiences; you'll find advice, solutions and the strength to face challenges together.

The Northumberland LA peer group are Cheryl Auld, Justine Overton, Hannah Williamson, Alison Hawkins, Nadine Fielding, Mark Burgess, Keri Dowdney, Sarah Smith, Mark Phillips, Clare Scott and Gavin Johnston.

PART 3

What next?

18

What next?

We have talked often and at some length about the need for a cultural shift in our approaches to supporting leaders in our education system with the intention of making access to support part of the preparation for becoming a headteacher.

Our mission

Our mission here is twofold:

1. to have a significant positive impact on the retention figures for school leaders, providing leaders with the support that they need so that in challenging times they are able to survive in their role;
2. to provide leaders with the support and tools that enable them to meet the challenges of their role and stay connected to their sense of purpose and therefore more regularly notice and acknowledge the joy of their role, enabling them to thrive across the duration of what could and should be lengthy careers impacting on the lives of thousands of young people in their communities.

We have had significant experience in this area, to date having worked with 4,500 plus leaders in the English education system, with 100 per cent of them reporting that they have found it beneficial and would recommend our type of support to another headteacher/leader. We have improved well-being, reduced stress and anxiety and impact on the self-perception leaders have about their ability to lead.

Our mission has been achieved at a grassroots level, and we are enormously grateful to those local authorities, multi-academy trusts and partners who recognise the need to take a more intentional and sustainable approach to supporting the well-being of those headteachers – past, present and future – for whom they are responsible and who give of themselves so tirelessly on behalf of those young people and adults within their communities. It is through these partnerships and collaborations that we have been able to fulfil our mission and to go some way to creating a network and system of support.

Despite ongoing conversations with the DfE highlighting both the need and the solutions that are possible, the reality is that our work has been independent of DfE support. This is an observation rather than a criticism; however, we recognise that we are only going to be able to truly shift the culture in our system with system-level approaches and we believe that the DfE has the responsibility for creating the policy environment and funding to ensure that we can truly create a culture of positive impact on *all* leaders in our education system, for the benefit of those leaders and the young people and adults in their communities.

We believe that the responsibility of the DfE goes beyond establishing the policy, frameworks and standards to prepare leaders for headship, through leadership development programmes (national professional qualifications (NPQs)), and that it should include establishing the policy, frameworks and environment in which leaders are enabled to thrive in their role.

A suite of support

We propose that the DfE enable all leaders who are preparing for headship be provided with an entitlement to a suite of support that includes the following elements:

- mentoring;
- coaching (in all its forms);
- peer support;
- supervision.

Through establishing policy, framework and standards that require all employers to offer such a suite of support there will be a clear expectation that the headteacher/leader will access it as needed.

The holistic nature of this entitlement is important. Too often we find that the impact that the different elements can have is misunderstood; this is especially true in regard to coaching, where there are a number of very different coaching approaches – some of which are wholly focused on developing and improving technical leadership skills. While this can be useful it tends to mirror and amplify the leadership development that is already provided for in the NPQs and is catered for adequately at local level by local authorities, multi-academy trusts and the numerous training providers.

It also demonstrates a misunderstanding of the issues that headteachers are grappling with and the issues that lead headteachers to resign their post:

> *Headteachers don't resign because they haven't got the skills required to be an effective community leader, they resign because* they don't believe *they have the skills to be an effective community leader.*
>
> James Pope

This is not an issue of technical leadership skill; it is an issue of self-belief – these are human issues, not issues of professionalism. Until we acknowledge this then we will continue to provide the wrong support and wonder why that support is not impacting positively on retention rates for leaders.

Funding

We propose that the DfE provides the funding in the short term (one to five years) to establish the entitlement and expectation of access for *all* headteachers. This funding should be provided to employers to pass to their headteacher with the intention that the headteacher is able to decide how the funding is spent to best suit their needs.

The DfE approach to this to date has been to leave this important work in the hands of local decision-makers. This creates two significant issues:

1. *inequity*: the ability of headteachers to access support of any kind is wholly dependent on access to funds. In a world of limited resources headteachers, as servant leaders, are highly unlikely to spend money on their own support. Where support is being accessed it is nearly always the case that funding and therefore permission has been granted by an external authority such as a local authority or a multi-academy trust. This is obviously great if you are a headteacher who works somewhere where this is the case … it is far less great if you are not and you have been left to make the decision to invest in yourself – it creates a significant inequity;

2. *defined support*: it is understandable for logistical and other reasons that where support is being provided the nature of that support is being dictated by the provider. While this is to be celebrated, it may not be the right support for that headteacher. The only person who can make that decision is the headteacher themselves (this, in itself, requires far better description and understanding of the impact of different types of support than currently exists in our system; in other words, you don't know what you don't know – although hopefully after reading this book you might have a better understanding).

The cost of this is not insignificant; however, we would propose that significantly more than this is currently being spent in the piecemeal approaches we have across our system. Furthermore, the cost pales into insignificance if we include:

- the ongoing cost to the system of having to replace headteachers who are resigning, often lost to the education system altogether;
- the cost of providing temporary arrangements to cover headteachers and leaders who are taking leave of absence due to stress and anxiety;
- the hidden cost of leaders whose stress and anxiety is such that they are unable to perform at their best.

We will continue to work with our partners to campaign for the above on behalf of all headteachers – past, present and future.

Creative approaches

In the meantime, we continue to create innovative approaches to a self-sustaining system:

1. *through our highly impactful peer support approach*: creating local networks of support across the country, alongside our national network, these local networks provide headteachers/leaders with access to an ongoing supportive peer group with no cost beyond the set-up and the time required to keep them running;
2. *through the open sharing of our impactful nine steps programme in our peer support, coaching programmes, our app and indeed in this book*: these practical, simple strategies and actions have a demonstrable impact on enabling headteachers and leaders to maintain and sustain healthy levels of well-being;

3. *through the provision of our HeadsUp4HTs app*: using AI and our learning through working with thousands of headteachers and leaders to provide leaders with real-time access to HeadsUp4HTs approaches and coaching sessions. This means headteachers and leaders can receive support when they need it, every day if necessary, for an annual cost that is less than two coaching sessions.

These approaches, created in a world where financial resources are lacking, have the additional benefit of being low-cost solutions compared to pure coaching and mentoring models. This is significant as it could severely reduce the cost of our second proposal to the DfE (see above); collectively they create a self-sustaining system which means the costs are not ongoing in the same way as they would be compared to a commitment to coaching/mentoring/supervision provision.

Our ambition

Our ambition in our work goes beyond providing effective well-being support to leaders (as important as this to our mission). In the HeadsUp4HTs network we are all passionate educators and passionate about education. Beyond the well-being support, our approaches have significant value-add in the following areas:

1. *purposeful leaders*: our well-being work, with its focus on purpose, means HeadsUp4HTs headteachers are not only healthier from a well-being point of view, they also happen to be better leaders;
2. *transformational leaders*: leaders with a strong sense of purpose and a high sense of well-being also have the capacity to engage in longer-term strategic development and transformation (not swamped with the day job);
3. *system leaders*: leaders who have a strong connection to their purpose are reinvigorated – the 'fire in the belly' – and are more likely to want to and have the capacity to engage in dialogue and discussion about the purpose of education locally, regionally and nationally;
4. *innovative change leaders*: 'well' leaders are also more likely to have the capacity for innovation and creativity, therefore creating the conditions and environment in which we can transform our education system at a grassroots level in order to meet the challenges of a rapidly changing world.

Index

Zeitfracht Medien GmbH
Ferdinand-Jühlke-Straße 7
99095 Erfurt, Deutschland
produktsicherheit@kolibri360.de